CAKES
& PASTRIES

CAKES
& PASTRIES

NOTES

1. Unless otherwise specified, all recipes serve four persons.

2. All spoon measurements are level and based on metric spoons: 1 teaspoon = 5ml, 1 tablespoon = 15ml. Spoon measures can be bought in both imperial and metric sizes to give accurate measurement of small quantities.

3. All eggs are size 2 or 3 unless otherwise stated.

4. All sugar is granulated unless otherwise stated.

5. Preparation times are an average calculated during recipe testing.

6. Metric and imperial measurements have been calculated separately. Use one set of measurements only as they are not exact equivalents.

7. Cooking times may vary slightly depending on the individual oven. Dishes should be placed in the centre of the oven unless otherwise specified.

8. Always preheat the oven or grill to the specified temperature.

ACKNOWLEDGMENTS
Compiled and edited by Norma MacMillan
Art Directors: Sara Kidd and Bobbie Colegate-Stone
Designer: Carole Perks
Production: Alyssum Ross
Special Photography: Clive Streeter
Stylist: Marian Price
Home Economist: Carole Handslip
Cover Photography: Clive Streeter
Illustrations: Anne Ormerod

This edition first published in 1990
exclusively for Marks and Spencer plc
by arrangement with
the Octopus Publishing Group
Michelin House, 81 Fulham Road, London SW3 6RB

ISBN 0 706 440 056

Produced by Mandarin Offset
Printed and bound in Hong Kong

CONTENTS

FAMILY CAKES

*The pleasures of making a cake are many – the wonderful
smells, your family's anticipation of enjoying a delicious
treat, and the satisfaction of having created something
special for those you love. Added to this is knowing just
what ingredients have been used, and being able to ensure
that they are the best. In this chapter are recipes for plain
and simple cakes, sandwich and layer cakes, with a
variety of fillings, icings and frostings, fruit and nut
cakes and a Swiss roll.*

WALNUT LAYER CAKE

This is traditionally a very sweet cake and, if preferred, the smaller quantity of sugar may be used.

225g (8oz) butter, at room temperature, or soft tub
margarine
275–350g (10–12oz) caster sugar
225g (8oz) plain flour
1 tablespoon baking powder
pinch of salt
250ml (8floz) milk
4 egg whites
75–100g (3–4oz) shelled walnuts, chopped
¼ teaspoon vanilla essence (optional)
9 walnut halves, to decorate
CHOCOLATE SOURED CREAM FROSTING:
75g (3oz) plain chocolate, broken into pieces
2 tablespoons water
225g (8oz) icing sugar
about 75 ml (3floz) soured cream

Preparation time: 1 hour, plus cooling
Cooking time: 30 minutes
Oven: 180°C, 350°F, Gas Mark 4

1. Grease and line three 20cm (8 inch) sandwich tins.
2. Cream the fat and sugar together until light and fluffy. Sift together the flour, baking powder and salt and mix them into the creamed mixture alternately with the milk, a third at a time. Whisk the egg whites until stiff but still moist, and fold into the mixture, alternating with the chopped nuts. Flavour with the vanilla if liked.
3. Divide the mixture between the tins and bake in a preheated oven for about 30 minutes or until springy to the touch.
4. To make the frosting, put the chocolate in a bowl with the water over a saucepan of simmering water. The hot water must not touch the bottom of the bowl. When soft, stir until smooth and creamy. Sift the icing sugar into a bowl and gradually stir in 2 tablespoons soured cream. Mix in the melted chocolate and add a little more soured cream to give a thick coating consistency.
5. Spread the cake layers with some of the frosting, sandwich together and swirl the remainder over the top and sides of the cake. Decorate with walnut halves.

MAKES A 20CM (8 INCH) THREE-LAYER CAKE
(10 SLICES)
Nutrition content per serving   Carbohydrate: 80g   Fat: 29g
Fibre: 1.4g   Kilocalories: 586

CARDAMOM CREAM CAKE

100g (4oz) butter
225g (8oz) caster sugar
2 teaspoons ground cardamom
1 egg, beaten
150ml (¼ pint) single cream
350g (12oz) self-raising flour
thinly pared lemon rind, to decorate
ICING:
about 1 tablespoon lemon juice
100g (4oz) icing sugar, sifted

Preparation time: 25 minutes, plus cooling
Cooking time: 40–45 minutes
Oven: 180°C, 350°F, Gas Mark 4

1. Well grease a 23cm (9 inch) ring mould and dust with flour.
2. Melt the butter and pour over the sugar in a bowl. Beat in the cardamom, egg and cream, then stir in the sifted flour. Turn into the prepared mould and level off.
3. Bake in a preheated oven for 40–45 minutes or until well risen and pale golden. Leave in the mould for 2 minutes, then turn out on to a wire tray to cool.
4. To make the icing, blend the lemon juice into the icing sugar to make a thick, flowing consistency. Spoon over the top of the cake, allowing it to run down the sides.
5. Cut the lemon rind into long strips. Put into a basin, cover with boiling water and leave for 5 minutes, then drain and dry well. Decorate the top of the cake with these strips.

SERVES 8
Nutrition content per serving   Carbohydrate: 77g   Fat: 5g
Fibre: 2g   Kilocalories: 353

Cardamom cream cake (top); Walnut layer cake

ALMOND GENOESE SANDWICH

65g (2½oz) plain flour
15g (½oz) cornflour
3 eggs
75g (3oz) caster sugar
40g (1½oz) butter, melted
a few drops of almond essence
DECORATION:
300ml (½ pint) double or whipping cream
175g (6oz) raspberry or other jam
1–2 kiwi fruit
toasted flaked almonds

Preparation time: about 25 minutes
Cooking time: 20–25 minutes
Oven: 190°C, 375°F, Gas Mark 5

1. Grease and line two 20cm (8 inch) sandwich cake tins – round or square.
2. Sift the flour and cornflour together twice.
3. Whisk the eggs and sugar together until very thick and pale and the whisk leaves a trail when it is lifted out. (Place the bowl over a pan of hot water if not whisking with an electric beater.)
4. Fold in most of the sifted flour, then add the cooled but still liquid butter and essence and finally the remaining flour, folding quickly and evenly and using a metal spoon.
5. Pour into the prepared tins and level out, making sure there is plenty of mixture in the corners of square tins.
6. Place in a preheated oven and bake for 20–25 minutes, until well risen and just firm to the touch.
7. Turn out on to a wire tray to cool, then peel off the paper.
8. For the decoration: whip the cream until stiff. Soften the jam and fold evenly through half of the cream.
9. Use the raspberry cream to sandwich the cakes together. Spread half of the remaining cream over the top of the cake and mark into swirls. Pipe the remaining cream round the edge, and decorate with the kiwi fruit and almonds.

MAKES A 20CM (8 INCH) SANDWICH CAKE (8 SLICES)
Nutrition content per serving   Carbohydrate: 27g   Fat: 16g
Fibre: 1g   Kilocalories: 258

DUNDEE CAKE

175g (6oz) butter, at room temperature
175g (6oz) soft brown sugar
3 eggs, lightly beaten
175g (6oz) plain flour
25g (1oz) ground almonds
1 teaspoon baking powder
225g (8oz) sultanas
225g (8oz) currants
75g (3oz) chopped mixed peel
75g (3oz) glacé cherries, halved
1 teaspoon finely grated lemon rind
1½ tablespoons lemon juice
about 50 split blanched almonds

Preparation time: 25 minutes
Cooking time: 2½ hours
Oven: 180°C, 350°F, Gas Mark 4; then
150°C, 300°F, Gas Mark 2

1. Well grease an 18cm (7 inch) round cake tin and line the bottom and sides with greased greaseproof paper.
2. Cream the butter and sugar together until light and fluffy. Gradually beat in the eggs, adding a tablespoon of the flour with the last amount. Fold in the almonds. Sift in the remaining flour and baking powder and fold into the creamed mixture with the dried fruit, peel, cherries, lemon rind and juice.
3. Turn into the prepared tin and level off. Arrange the almonds on the top of the cake and brush with a little egg white; you can get enough for this by brushing inside the egg shells.
4. Bake in a preheated oven for 1 hour, then reduce the temperature to cool and bake for a further 1½ hours or until a skewer inserted into the centre comes out clean.
5. Leave in the tin for 10 minutes, then carefully turn out on to a wire tray to cool.

MAKES AN 18CM (7 INCH) ROUND CAKE (8 SLICES)
Nutrition content per serving   Carbohydrate: 91g   Fat: 7g
Fibre: 5g   Kilocalories: 577

Almond genoese sandwich (top); Dundee cake

CHOCOLATE POTATO LAYER CAKE

The unlikely combination of mashed potato and chocolate makes a light and moist cake, with the rum adding a richness of flavour.

100g (4oz) hot mashed potato
2 tablespoons double cream
65g (2½oz) unsalted butter, at room temperature
200g (7oz) caster sugar
50g (2oz) plain chocolate, melted
¾ teaspoon bicarbonate of soda
2 tablespoons water
3 eggs, separated
100g (4oz) plain flour
1 teaspoon baking powder
¼ teaspoon salt
4 tablespoons milk
1½ teaspoons rum
chocolate triangles, to decorate
RUM-COCOA ICING:
40g (1½oz) unsalted butter
225g (8oz) icing sugar
2 tablespoons cocoa powder
¼ teaspoon salt
1 tablespoon rum
1½ tablespoons strong black coffee

Preparation time: 55 minutes, plus cooling
Cooking time: 30 minutes
Oven: 190°C, 375°F, Gas Mark 5

1. Butter two 18cm (7 inch) round cake tins and line with greaseproof paper. Brush the paper with melted butter and dust with flour.
2. Combine the mashed potato with the cream in a heatproof bowl. Keep hot over a pan of hot water. Beat the butter with the sugar until light and fluffy. Add the creamed potato and melted chocolate. Dissolve the bicarbonate of soda in the water and add to the potato mixture. Beat in the egg yolks one at a time.
3. Sift the flour, baking powder and salt together twice. Fold them into the mixture, adding alternately with the milk and rum.
4. Whisk the egg whites until stiff. Gently fold a third of the whites into the mixture, then fold in the rest.
5. Divide the mixture between the tins and bake in a preheated oven for 30 minutes or until a skewer inserted into the centre comes out clean. Remove from the oven and leave the cakes in the tins on a wire tray for 5 minutes before turning them out to cool completely.
6. To make the icing, beat the butter until pale and soft. Sift together the icing sugar, cocoa powder and salt and gradually incorporate into the butter. Stir in the rum and coffee.
7. Sandwich the two cakes together with some of the icing and use the rest to cover the top and sides of the cake. Decorate with chocolate triangles.

MAKES AN 18CM (7 INCH) SANDWICH CAKE (8 SLICES)
Nutrition content per serving   Carbohydrate: 73g   Fat: 18g
Fibre: 1g   Kilocalories: 461

HONEY & GINGER CAKE

In this recipe honey is used as part of the sugar content; this will keep the cake moist longer than the average plain cake.

225g (8oz) plain flour
1 teaspoon ground ginger
100g (4oz) butter or margarine
50g (2oz) caster sugar
100g (4oz) stem ginger, chopped
1 teaspoon bicarbonate of soda
150ml (¼ pint) milk
50g (2oz) clear honey
1 egg, beaten
1 tablespoon demerara sugar (optional)

Preparation time: 20 minutes
Cooking time: 1 hour
Oven: 170°C, 325°F, Gas Mark 3

1. Line the bottom of a 15cm (6 inch) cake tin.
2. Sift the flour and ground ginger into a mixing bowl. Cut the fat into the flour and rub in with the fingertips until the mixture resembles breadcrumbs. Mix in the caster sugar and stem ginger.
3. Dissolve the bicarbonate of soda in half the milk and stir into the honey. Make a well in the dry ingredients and stir in the milk mixture and beaten egg. Mix to a soft dropping consistency, adding more milk as required.
4. Turn into the prepared tin and level the top. Sprinkle over the demerara sugar, if using. Bake in the centre of a preheated oven for about 1 hour, until set and golden.
5. Allow to cool and shrink slightly, then remove from the tin and cool completely on a wire tray.

MAKES A 15CM (6 INCH) ROUND CAKE (6 SLICES)
Nutrition content per serving   Carbohydrate: 46g   Fat: 16g
Fibre: 1g   Kilocalories: 340

Chocolate potato layer cake (top); Honey & ginger cake

COCONUT FROSTED MARBLE CAKE

225g (8oz) self-raising flour
1½ teaspoons baking powder
175g (6oz) caster sugar
175g (6oz) soft tub margarine
3 eggs
3 tablespoons milk
grated rind of 1 lemon
1 tablespoon cocoa powder, sifted
50g (2oz) shredded coconut, toasted, to decorate
SEVEN-MINUTE FROSTING:
1 egg white
150g (5oz) caster sugar
pinch of salt
2 tablespoons water
pinch of cream of tartar

Preparation time: about 40 minutes
Cooking time: about 45 minutes
Oven: 170°C, 325°F, Gas Mark 3

1. Grease a 1.1 litre (2 pint) ring mould and dust the inside lightly with flour.
2. Sift the flour and baking powder into a bowl. Add the sugar, margarine, eggs and milk and beat well for about 2 minutes, until smooth and evenly blended.
3. Put half of the mixture into another bowl and beat in the lemon rind.
4. Add the cocoa to the first half of the mixture and beat until evenly distributed.
5. Put alternate tablespoons of the mixtures into the ring mould to give a marbled effect. Level the top.
6. Place in a preheated oven and bake for about 45 minutes or until well risen and firm to the touch.
7. Cool for a minute or so in the mould, then turn out carefully on to a wire tray and leave until cold.
8. To make the frosting, put all the ingredients into a heatproof bowl and mix lightly. Place the bowl over a saucepan of gently simmering water and beat well, preferably with a hand-held electric mixer, until thick enough to stand in peaks. Remove from the heat and use at once.

9. Spread and swirl the frosting over the ring cake to cover it completely. Sprinkle quickly with the toasted coconut as this icing tends to set very quickly. Leave until set before serving.

SERVES 8
Nutrition content per serving   Carbohydrate: 65g   Fat: 25g
Fibre: 3g   Kilocalories: 493

GLAZED NUT TEABREAD

100g (4oz) butter, at room temperature
100g (4oz) soft light brown sugar
2 eggs, beaten
100g (4oz) shelled mixed nuts, finely chopped
120ml (4floz) milk
225g (8oz) self-raising flour
2 teaspoons ground cinnamon
25g (1oz) shelled whole nuts, to decorate
1 tablespoon warmed honey, to glaze

Preparation time: 20 minutes
Cooking time: 50–55 minutes
Oven: 180°C, 350°F, Gas Mark 4

1. Grease and line the bottom of a 1kg (2lb) loaf tin.
2. Cream the butter and sugar together until light and fluffy.
3. Beat in the eggs, a little at a time.
4. Stir in the nuts and milk. Sift the flour and cinnamon into the bowl, then fold in lightly using a metal spoon.
5. Turn the mixture into the prepared tin and smooth over the top.
6. Arrange a cluster of whole nuts along the centre of the loaf, then place the tin on a baking sheet.
7. Bake in a preheated oven for 50–55 minutes, until the cake is deep golden brown and springs back when pressed with the fingers.
8. Cool in the tin for 5 minutes, then turn out on to a wire tray. Brush with the warmed honey and leave to cool.

MAKES A LARGE LOAF-SHAPED CAKE (12 SLICES)
Nutrition content per serving   Carbohydrate: 25g   Fat: 13g
Fibre: 2g   Kilocalories: 234

Below: Glazed nut teabread
Opposite: Coconut frosted marble cake

APRICOT BUTTERSCOTCH SANDWICH

175g (6oz) butter or margarine, at room temperature
75g (3oz) light soft brown sugar
75g (3oz) dark soft brown sugar
3 eggs, beaten
175g (6oz) self-raising flour, sifted
1 tablespoon black treacle
1 tablespoon lemon juice
FILLING:
1 × 425g (15oz) can apricot halves
150ml (¼ pint) double or whipping cream
3 tablespoons milk or medium white wine

Preparation time: 30 minutes
Cooking time: 20–25 minutes
Oven: 190°C, 375°F, Gas Mark 5

1. Grease and line two 20 cm (8 inch) square sandwich cake tins.
2. Cream the butter or margarine and sugars together until light and fluffy. Beat in the eggs, a little at a time. Fold in the flour with a metal spoon until evenly mixed, then beat in the black treacle and lemon juice.
3. Divide the mixture between the tins, levelling the tops and making sure there is sufficient mixture in the corners of the tins.
4. Place in a preheated oven and bake for about 20 minutes or until well risen, golden brown and just firm to the touch. Turn out on to a wire tray and leave to cool. Peel off the paper.
5. For the filling: drain the apricots and chop half of them. Cut each of the remaining apricot halves into quarters.
6. Whip the cream and milk or wine together until stiff. Put almost half into a piping bag fitted with a 1 cm (⅓ inch) plain vegetable nozzle. Fold the remainder into the chopped apricots.
7. Use the apricot cream to sandwich the cakes together and place on a serving plate.
8. Pipe lines of cream over the top of the cake and decorate with pieces of apricot. Serve as soon as possible.

**MAKES A 20CM (8 INCH) SQUARE SANDWICH CAKE
(8 SLICES)**
Nutrition content per serving   Carbohydrate: 53g   Fat: 30g
Fibre: 2g   Kilocalories: 489

CHOCOLATE PEPPERMINT SWISS ROLL

2 eggs
50g (2oz) caster sugar
50g (2oz) self-raising flour, less 1 tablespoon
1 tablespoon cocoa powder
extra caster sugar, for dredging
FILLING:
50g (2oz) butter, at room temperature
75g (3oz) icing sugar, sifted
few drops of peppermint essence

Preparation time: 30 minutes, plus cooling
Cooking time: 7–10 minutes
Oven: 200°C, 400°F, Gas Mark 6

1. Grease and line an 18 × 28cm (7 × 11 inch) Swiss roll tin.
2. Whisk the eggs and sugar together until they are light and creamy and the whisk leaves a trail when it is lifted out. (Place the bowl over a pan of hot water if not whisking with an electric beater.) Sift the flour and cocoa, then fold into the mixture. Turn into the tin and level off.
3. Bake in a preheated oven for 7–10 minutes, until the cake springs back when lightly pressed with the fingertips.
4. Turn out on to a piece of greaseproof paper dredged with caster sugar. Trim off the edges and quickly roll up the cake with the paper inside. Allow to cool.
5. Cream the butter and icing sugar together, then beat in the peppermint essence.
6. Unroll the cake, removing the greaseproof paper, spread with the peppermint butter cream, then re-roll. Dredge the outside of the roll with caster sugar before serving.

SERVES 6
Nutrition content per serving   Carbohydrate: 28g   Fat: 9g
Fibre: trace   Kilocalories: 206

Apricot butterscotch sandwich (top); Chocolate peppermint Swiss roll

NORWEGIAN APPLE CAKE

2 eggs
250g (9oz) caster sugar
100g (4oz) butter
150ml (¼ pint) top of the milk or creamy milk
175g (6oz) plain flour
1 tablespoon baking powder
3–4 Bramley cooking apples

Preparation time: 30 minutes
Cooking time: 20–25 minutes
Oven: 200°C, 400°F, Gas Mark 6

1. Grease and flour a 20 × 30cm (8 × 12 inch) roasting tin.
2. Whisk the eggs and 225g (8oz) of the sugar until the mixture is thick and creamy and the whisk leaves a trail when it is lifted out. (Place the bowl over a pan of hot water if not whisking with an electric beater.)
3. Put the butter and milk into a pan. Bring to the boil and stir, still boiling, into the eggs and sugar. Sift in the flour and baking powder and fold carefully into the mixture so that there are no lumps of flour. Pour the mixture into the prepared roasting tin.
4. Peel, core and slice the apples; arrange them over the cake mixture. Sprinkle with the remaining sugar.
5. Bake in a preheated oven for 20–25 minutes, until well risen and golden brown. Cool in the tin, then cut into slices to serve.

MAKES A 20 × 30CM (8 × 12 INCH) CAKE (12 SLICES)
Nutrition content per serving   Carbohydrate: 40g   Fat: 9g
Fibre: 2g   Kilocalories: 241

WELSH HONEY CAKE

This honey cake with its meringue topping can be served for tea or as a dessert for lunch.

225g (8oz) plain flour
½ teaspoon bicarbonate of soda
1 teaspoon ground cinnamon
100g (4oz) butter, at room temperature
100g (4oz) soft brown sugar
3 eggs, separated
100g (4oz) honey, warmed
about 2 tablespoons warm water
TOPPING:
50g (2oz) caster sugar
1 tablespoon warm honey

Preparation time: 30 minutes, plus cooling
Cooking time: 55–60 minutes
Oven: 200°C, 400°F, Gas Mark 6; then
190°C, 375°F, Gas Mark 5; then
170°C, 325°F, Gas Mark 3

1. Grease a 20cm (8 inch) round cake tin with a removable base.
2. Sift the flour with the bicarbonate of soda and cinnamon. Cream the butter and brown sugar together until light and fluffy. Beat in the egg yolks gradually and then the warmed honey. Fold in the flour, adding a little warm water if the mixture gets too stiff. Beat one egg white until stiff but not too dry and fold it in lightly.
3. Turn the mixture into the prepared tin. Bake in a preheated oven for 15 minutes, then lower the heat and bake for a further 20–30 minutes. Remove from the oven and allow the cake to shrink slightly before turning it out.
4. Beat the remaining 2 egg whites until stiff. Fold in the caster sugar quickly and lightly.
5. Put the cake on a baking sheet and brush it all over with warmed honey. Swirl the meringue over with a palette knife, drawing it up in points.
6. Turn the oven down again, return the cake to it and bake for 15 minutes or until the meringue is set and delicately coloured. Serve cold.

MAKES A 20CM (8 INCH) ROUND CAKE (8 SLICES)
Nutrition content per serving   Carbohydrate: 52g   Fat: 13g
Fibre: 1g   Kilocalories: 334

Norwegian apple cake; Welsh honey cake

CUMBRIAN LEMON CAKE

The first Englishmen to enjoy oranges and lemons were the Crusaders, who wintered with Richard Coeur de Lion in Jaffa in 1191–2.

100g (4oz) butter, at room temperature
50g (2oz) lard
150g (5oz) caster sugar
2 eggs (size 1)
225g (8oz) self-raising flour
2 tablespoons lemon juice
grated rind of 1 lemon
50g (2oz) candied lemon peel, chopped
1 tablespoon milk (optional)
TO FINISH:
icing sugar
lemon curd

Preparation time: 25 minutes
Cooking time: 1–1½ hours
Oven: 180°C, 350°F, Gas Mark 4

1. Lightly butter an 18cm (7 inch) round cake tin with a removable base.
2. Cream the butter, lard and sugar together until light and fluffy. Add the eggs, one at a time, with about 1 tablespoon of flour for each, and mix in thoroughly. Fold in the rest of the flour.
3. Add the lemon juice, the finely grated rind and the chopped candied lemon peel. Mix well, and only add the milk if the mixture seems too stiff. It should be of firm, dropping consistency.
4. Pour into the prepared tin and bake in the centre of a preheated oven for about 1 hour. Check that it

is cooked through by inserting a small skewer, which will come out clean if the cake is ready. If necessary, continue cooking for up to a further 30 minutes.
5. Leave to cool in the tin for 5 minutes before removing and cooling on a wire tray.
6. To serve, the cake can simply be sprinkled with sifted icing sugar or cut into two layers and sandwiched with lemon curd.

MAKES AN 18CM (7 INCH) ROUND CAKE (8 SLICES)
Nutrition content per serving   Carbohydrate: 44g   Fat: 19g
Fibre: 1g   Kilocalories: 350

ORANGE KUGELHUPF

225g (8oz) butter, at room temperature
225g (8oz) caster sugar
3 eggs
225g (8oz) self-raising flour, sifted
grated rind of 1½–2 oranges
50g (2oz) chopped mixed peel
ORANGE SYRUP:
50g (2oz) icing sugar, sifted
5 tablespoons orange juice
TOPPING:
finely pared rind of 1 orange
150ml (¼ pint) water
50g (2oz) caster sugar
ORANGE GLACÉ ICING:
100g (4oz) icing sugar, sifted
about 1 tablespoon orange juice
orange food colouring

Preparation time: about 45 minutes, plus 24 hours' standing
Cooking time: about 1 hour
Oven: 190°C, 375°F, Gas Mark 5

1. Grease a 1.75 litre (3 pint) kugelhupf fancy ring mould or other ring mould with melted lard or butter.
2. Cream the butter and sugar together until light and fluffy.
3. Beat in the eggs one at a time following each with a spoonful of the flour. Fold in the remainder of the flour followed by the orange rind and mixed peel.
4. Turn into the prepared tin and level the top. Stand the tin on a baking sheet. Place in a preheated oven and bake for about 1 hour or until well risen and firm to the touch. Turn out on to a wire tray.
5. For the orange syrup: blend the icing sugar and orange juice together and spoon over the cake while it is still warm. When cold, wrap in foil or store in an airtight container for 24 hours before proceeding.

6. For the topping: cut the orange rind into julienne strips and put into a saucepan. Add the water and simmer for 5 minutes. Add the sugar, stir until dissolved then boil until syrupy. Remove the orange rind and drain on a paper towel.
7. For the glacé icing: put the icing sugar into a bowl and gradually work in the orange juice and a few drops of orange colouring to give a spreading consistency.
8. Stand the cake on a plate and spoon and spread the icing over the top, allowing it to run over the edge and down the sides. Just before it sets, sprinkle with the orange rind.

Variation: Lemon rind and juice can be used in place of orange to make a lemon version, but increase the sugar content to 100g (4oz) for the syrup.

SERVES 12
*Nutrition content per serving   Carbohydrate: 56g   Fat: 17g
Fibre: 1g   Kilocalories: 379*

*Above: Orange kugelhupf
Opposite: Cumbrian lemon cake*

CRYSTALLIZED FRUIT CAKE

This cake is rich and moist. It makes a delightful alternative to the traditional Christmas cake, which many people find too heavy.

175g (6oz) butter, at room temperature
175g (6oz) caster sugar
3 eggs, beaten
50g (2oz) blanched almonds, chopped
50g (2oz) glacé cherries, chopped
25g (1oz) crystallized ginger, chopped
25g (1oz) crystallized pineapple, chopped
50g (2oz) dried apricots, chopped
50g (2oz) ground almonds
175g (6oz) plain flour
½ teaspoon baking powder
TOPPING:
2 tablespoons apricot jam
50g (2oz) mixed crystallized chopped fruit

Preparation time: 35 minutes
Cooking time: 2½ hours
Oven: 150°C, 300°F, Gas Mark 2

1. Grease and line an 18cm (7 inch) round cake tin.
2. Cream the butter and sugar together until light and fluffy.
3. Beat in the eggs, a little at a time.
4. Stir in the chopped almonds, cherries, ginger, pineapple and apricots.
5. Add the ground almonds. Sift the flour and baking powder into the bowl, then fold into the mixture lightly with a metal spoon until evenly mixed.
6. Place the mixture in the prepared tin and smooth over the top.
7. Bake in a preheated oven for 2½ hours, until the cake is light golden and springs back when pressed with the fingers.
8. Leave to cool in the tin for 30 minutes, then turn out, remove the paper and cool on a wire tray.
9. Heat the apricot jam with 1 tablespoon of water, add the chopped crystallized fruit and spread evenly over the top of the cake.

Variation: To make a light buttery fruit cake, replace the cherries, ginger, pineapple and apricots with 175g (6oz) mixed dried fruit or one fruit of your choice. Sprinkle the top of the cake with 50g (2oz) chopped nuts before baking it.

MAKES AN 18CM (7 INCH) ROUND CAKE (8 SLICES)
Nutrition content per serving   Carbohydrate: 62g   Fat: 27g
Fibre: 4g   Kilocalories: 510

ST CLEMENT'S CAKE

175g (6oz) butter or margarine, at room temperature
175g (6oz) caster sugar
3 eggs, beaten
grated rind of 1 lemon
175g (6oz) self-raising flour
orange and lemon jelly slices, to decorate
ICING:
225g (8oz) icing sugar, sifted
75g (3oz) butter, at room temperature
1 teaspoon grated orange rind
2 tablespoons orange juice
few drops of orange food colouring

Preparation time: 25 minutes
Cooking time: 30 minutes
Oven: 180°C, 350°F, Gas Mark 4

1. Grease and line the bottom of two 20cm (8 inch) sandwich cake tins.
2. Cream the butter or margarine and sugar together until light and fluffy.
3. Beat in the eggs, a little at a time.
4. Stir in the lemon rind. Add the flour and fold in lightly with a metal spoon until evenly mixed.
5. Divide the mixture between the two prepared tins. Smooth the top of each with the back of a spoon.
6. Bake in a preheated oven for 30 minutes, until the cakes are golden brown and spring back when pressed with the fingers. Turn out and leave to cool on a wire tray.
7. Place all the icing ingredients in a bowl. Mix, then beat for 2 minutes until light and creamy.
8. Sandwich the two cakes together with one-third of the icing. Spread the remaining icing over the top and sides of the cake. Mark with a fork in wavy lines.
9. Decorate with orange and lemon jelly slices.

MAKES A 20CM (8 INCH) SANDWICH CAKE (8 SLICES)
Nutrition content per serving   Carbohydrate: 69g   Fat: 28g
Fibre: 1g   Kilocalories: 534

Crystallized fruit cake; St Clement's cake (top)

AMERICAN FRUIT & NUT CAKE

175g (6oz) stoned 'no-need-to-soak' prunes, finely
chopped
100g (4oz) dried apricot halves, finely chopped
6 tablespoons dark rum
175g (6oz) butter or margarine, at room temperature
175g (6oz) dark soft brown sugar
3 eggs
100g (4oz) wholewheat flour
100g (4oz) plain flour
¾ teaspoon baking powder
¾ teaspoon ground allspice
¼ teaspoon ground ginger
100g (4oz) shelled mixed nuts (such as almonds,
hazelnuts, walnuts, pecans), chopped
175g (6oz) raisins
grated rind of 1 lemon
grated rind of 1 orange
1 tablespoon black treacle
TOPPING:
about 4 tablespoons redcurrant jelly, melted
selection of shelled mixed nuts (such as Brazils,
pecans, almonds, walnuts)
a few 'no-need-to-soak' prunes
halved glacé cherries

Preparation time: 30 minutes
Cooking time: 1¾–2 hours
Oven: 150°C, 300°F, Gas Mark 2

1. Put the prunes and apricots into a bowl with the rum. Leave to soak for about 15 minutes while preparing the rest of the ingredients.
2. Line the sides of a 20cm (8 inch) spring release cake tin fitted with a tubular base with 2 strips of non-stick silicone or greased greaseproof paper.
3. Cream the fat and sugar together until light and fluffy.
4. Beat in the eggs, one at a time, following each with 1 tablespoon of wholewheat flour.
5. Sift the plain flour with the baking powder and spices and fold into the mixture with the remaining wholewheat flour.
6. Add all the other ingredients including the soaked prunes and apricots (plus any excess liquid in the bowl) and mix well.

7. Turn into the tin and level the top. Tie a treble thickness piece of newspaper around the outside of the tin.
8. Place in a preheated oven and bake for 1¾–2 hours or until a skewer inserted in the cake comes out clean. Leave in the tin until cold, then remove carefully and peel off the lining paper.
9. For the topping: brush the cake with the redcurrant jelly, then arrange an attractive decoration of nuts, prunes and cherries on the top. Brush again with more jelly and leave to set.

MAKES A 20CM (8 INCH) RING CAKE (14 OR MORE
SLICES)
Nutrition content per serving   Carbohydrate: 41g   Fat: 17g
Fibre: 5g   Kilocalories: 336

COCONUT TEACAKE

This cake from the West Indies is surprisingly moist
and rich despite its lack of eggs and fat.

150g (5oz) desiccated coconut
450ml (¾ pint) milk
400g (14oz) plain flour
2 teaspoons baking powder
¼ teaspoon ground cloves
¼ teaspoon ground cinnamon
½ teaspoon salt
275g (10oz) caster sugar

Preparation time: 10 minutes, plus soaking
Cooking time: 1¼–1½ hours
Oven: 180°C, 350°F, Gas Mark 4

1. Grease a 900g (2lb) loaf tin.
2. Mix together the coconut and milk. Leave to soak for 30 minutes.
3. Sift the flour, baking powder, cloves, cinnamon and salt into a bowl. Stir in the sugar.
4. Mix the coconut and milk into the dry ingredients to make a soft batter.
5. Pour the mixture into the prepared tin. Smooth over the top.
6. Bake in a preheated oven for 1¼–1½ hours, until light golden and firm to the touch.
7. Turn out and cool on a wire tray. Serve sliced and buttered.

MAKES A LARGE LOAF-SHAPED CAKE (12 SLICES)
Nutrition content per serving   Carbohydrate: 53g   Fat: 10g
Fibre: 4g   Kilocalories: 306

American fruit & nut cake (top); Coconut teacake

COFFEE FUDGE CAKE

150g (5oz) butter or margarine, at room temperature
150g (5oz) soft brown sugar
3 eggs
150g (5oz) self-raising flour, sifted
1 tablespoon coffee essence or very strong black coffee
1 tablespoon black treacle
orange and lemon jelly slices, chopped almonds or
toasted hazelnuts, to decorate
ICING:
100g (4oz) butter
225g (8oz) icing sugar, sifted
1 tablespoon coffee essence or very strong black coffee
1 tablespoon black treacle

Preparation time: 15 minutes
Cooking time: 20–25 minutes
Oven: 190°C, 375°F, Gas Mark 5

1. Grease and line the bottoms of two 20cm (8 inch) cake tins and dredge with flour.
2. Cream together the fat and sugar until very light and fluffy. Beat in the eggs one at a time, following each with a spoonful of the flour. Using a metal spoon fold in the remaining flour alternately with the coffee and treacle.
3. Divide between the two tins, level the tops and bake in a preheated oven for about 20 minutes or until well risen and just firm to the touch. Turn out on to a wire tray and leave to cool.
4. To make the icing, cream the butter until soft, then gradually beat in the icing sugar alternating with the coffee and treacle to give a smooth spreading consistency. Use about one-third of the icing to sandwich the cakes together, then spread half of the remaining icing over the top of the cake and mark it into a pattern with a round-bladed knife. Put the rest of the icing into a piping bag fitted with a star nozzle and pipe horizontal lines of shells across the top of the cake.
5. Decorate with orange and lemon slices, almonds or toasted hazelnuts.

Variation: For a coffee cake, simply leave out the black treacle in both cake and icing.

MAKES A 20CM (8 INCH) SANDWICH CAKE (8 SLICES)
Nutrition content per serving   Carbohydrate: 65g   Fat: 28g
Fibre: 1g   Kilocalories: 515

ORANGE CURD CAKE

100g (4oz) self-raising flour
1 teaspoon baking powder
100g (4oz) caster sugar
100g (4oz) soft tub margarine
2 eggs
grated rind of 1 orange
FILLING AND DECORATION:
3 oranges
25g (1oz) caster sugar
175g (6oz) curd cheese
caster sugar, for dredging

Preparation time: 20–25 minutes
Cooking time: 30 minutes
Oven: 180°C, 350°F, Gas Mark 4

1. Grease and line the bottom of two 18cm (7inch) sandwich cake tins.
2. Place the flour, baking powder, sugar, margarine, eggs and orange rind in a bowl. Beat until light and fluffy.
3. Divide the mixture between the two prepared cake tins and smooth the tops.
4. Bake in a preheated oven for 30 minutes, until the cakes are golden brown and firm to the touch. Cool in the tins for 1 minute, then turn out and cool on a wire tray.
5. Cut the rind and all the white pith from the oranges, then cut into segments.
6. To make the filling, chop the segments from ½ orange, place in a bowl with the sugar and curd cheese and mix well together.
7. Sandwich the cakes together with three-quarters of the curd cheese filling, and spread the rest on the top of the cake. Arrange the remaining orange segments on the top and sprinkle with caster sugar.

MAKES AN 18CM (7 INCH) SANDWICH CAKE (8 SLICES)
Nutrition content per serving   Carbohydrate: 31g   Fat: 15g
Fibre: 1g   Kilocalories: 272

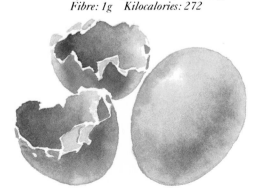

Coffee fudge cake (top); Orange curd cake

LUXURY CAKES & GATEAUX

When planning a menu for a dinner party or a celebration meal, a special dessert is called for. Luxury cakes and gâteaux are ideal for these occasions because they can be prepared ahead of time, leaving the cook free to concentrate on the other parts of the menu, and they are a wonderfully impressive finale. The cake recipes in this chapter are guaranteed to please your guests, and will tempt even the most sated to try a little bit.

ORANGE & COCONUT LAYER CAKE

50g (2oz) butter
75g (3oz) self-raising flour
3 eggs (size 1 or 2)
100g (4oz) caster sugar
finely grated rind of ½ orange
FILLING AND DECORATION:
250–275g (9–10oz) full fat soft cheese
2 tablespoons clear honey
1 tablespoon orange juice
25g (1oz) desiccated coconut
grated rind of ½ orange
1 tablespoon caster sugar
50g (2oz) desiccated coconut, toasted
2 medium oranges, peeled, sliced and halved

Preparation time: about 20 minutes
Cooking time: 20 minutes
Oven: 190°C, 375°F, Gas Mark 5

1. Grease and line a 28 × 18 × 4cm (11 × 7 × 1½ inch) rectangular tin.
2. Heat the butter gently until just melted, remove from the heat and leave to stand so the sediment sinks to the bottom. Sift the flour twice.
3. Whisk the eggs and sugar together with the orange rind until thick and pale and the whisk leaves a trail when it is lifted out. (Place the bowl over a pan of hot water if not whisking with an electric beater.)
4. Fold the sifted flour lightly and evenly through the mixture.
5. Carefully pour in the butter, without the sediment, and fold in carefully and lightly.
6. Turn into the prepared tin and bake in a preheated oven for about 20 minutes or until well risen, golden brown and firm to the touch. Turn out and cool on a wire tray. Remove the lining paper.
7. To make the filling, beat the cheese until light and fluffy, then beat in the honey and enough orange juice to give a soft spreading consistency.
8. Stir the coconut, orange rind and sugar into one-third of the cheese mixture.
9. Cut the cake in half lengthways and sandwich together with the orange cheese filling.
10. Use most of the remaining cheese mixture to mask the whole cake. Coat the sides evenly with the toasted coconut. Arrange the halved orange slices in a line down the centre of the top, and pipe the rest of the cheese mixture down the long edges.

MAKES A 28 × 8.5CM (11 × 3½ INCH) SANDWICH CAKE
(8 SLICES)
Nutrition content per serving Carbohydrate: 28g Fat: 29g
Fibre: 3g Kilocalories: 392

MALAKOFF GÂTEAU

1½–2 packets sponge finger biscuits
150g (5oz) blanched almonds, roughly chopped
100g (4oz) caster sugar
175g (6oz) butter, at room temperature
2 egg yolks
6 tablespoons brandy or dark rum
5 tablespoons milk
300ml (½ pint) whipping cream
toasted flaked almonds, to decorate

Preparation time: about 30 minutes, plus chilling

1. Grease and line a 450g (1lb) loaf tin. Cover the base with sponge finger biscuits.
2. Put the almonds and 50g (2oz) of the sugar in a small heavy-based pan and heat gently until the sugar turns a light caramel colour. Turn on to an oiled baking sheet, leave until cold and then crush this praline finely with a rolling pin or in a food processor.
3. Cream the butter with the remaining sugar until light and fluffy.
4. Beat in the egg yolks alternating with 3 tablespoons brandy or rum, then stir in the crushed praline.
5. Combine the milk and remaining brandy or rum and sprinkle 2 tablespoons over the biscuits in the tin, then spread with half the praline mixture.
6. Add a second layer of sponge finger biscuits, sprinkle with another 2 tablespoons milk mixture and cover with remaining praline mixture.
7. Lay a final layer of biscuits on top and sprinkle with the remaining milk mixture. Press down evenly, then cover with a sheet of greased greaseproof or non-stick silicone paper and then with foil.
8. If possible put a light weight on the cake and chill for at least 12 hours and preferably 24 hours.
9. Turn the gâteau out carefully on to a serving dish and gently peel off the paper.
10. Whip the cream and use some of it to mask the whole gâteau. Put the remainder in a piping bag fitted with a star nozzle and pipe diagonal lines on top of the gâteau. Sprinkle toasted almonds between the rows of cream.

SERVES 10
Nutrition content per serving Carbohydrate: 33g Fat: 36g
Fibre: 2g Kilocalories: 496

Orange & coconut layer cake; Malakoff gâteau

CROQUEMBOUCHE

This pyramid of choux buns is often served at an Italian wedding. The buns are filled with a delicious liqueur-flavoured cream and the whole thing is swathed in spun sugar.

CHOUX PASTE:
150g (5oz) plain flour
pinch of salt
300ml (½ pint) water
100g (4oz) butter
4 eggs, beaten
FILLING:
450ml (¾ pint) double cream
3 tablespoons orange liqueur
3 tablespoons icing sugar, sifted
SUGAR SYRUP:
350g (12oz) loaf or granulated sugar
150ml (¼ pint) water
5 teaspoons liquid glucose

Preparation time: about 40 minutes, plus spinning of sugar
Cooking time: about 1 hour
Oven: 220°C, 425°F, Gas Mark 7

1. For the choux paste: sift the flour and salt on to a sheet of greaseproof paper. Put the water in a pan with the butter, heat gently until the butter has melted and bring to the boil. When bubbling vigorously, remove from the heat. Add the flour all at once and beat well until the mixture forms a ball and leaves the sides of the pan clean.

2. Spread the paste out over the bottom of the pan and leave to cool until lukewarm.

3. Gradually beat in the eggs until the mixture is smooth and glossy and has a piping consistency. A hand-held electric mixer is ideal for this task.

4. Put the choux paste into a piping bag fitted with a plain 2cm (¾ inch) nozzle. Pipe the mixture into walnut-sized buns on greased baking sheets, keeping them well apart.

5. Place in a preheated oven and bake for 20–25 minutes or until well risen, golden brown and firm to the touch. Pierce each bun once to allow the steam to escape, return to the oven and bake for a further 2 minutes. Cool on a wire tray.

6. Whip the cream with the liqueur until stiff, then stir in the sugar. Use to fill the choux buns. A piping bag fitted with a 5mm (¼ inch) plain nozzle makes filling the buns easier than splitting and filling them; you can simply insert the nozzle in the steam escape hole.

7. Put half the sugar syrup ingredients into a heavy-based saucepan and heat gently until dissolved. Bring to the boil and boil rapidly until a temperature of 154°C (312°F) is reached on a sugar thermometer. Remove from the heat immediately.

8. Arrange a layer of choux buns on a silver board or dish, attaching them with a little sugar syrup. Then gradually build up the pyramid by dipping the base of each choux bun into the syrup so it will stick to the previous layer of buns. Continue to form a pyramid until the buns are all used.

9. Use the remaining sugar syrup ingredients and heat as before to the same temperature. Remove the pan from the heat and dip 2 forks into the syrup. Use only a small amount and wind it round and round the pyramid of buns so the sugar pulls into thin threads which stick to the buns. Repeat until all the syrup is used and a faint haze of spun sugar hangs all over the pyramid. If there is not enough spun sugar, then make up another half quantity and repeat the process. Serve as soon as possible.

SERVES 20
Nutrition content per serving   Carbohydrate: 29g   Fat: 15g
Fibre: 0g   Kilocalories: 252

Croquembouche

YULE LOG

4 eggs
100g (4oz) caster sugar
90g (3½oz) plain flour
15g (½oz) cocoa powder
25g (1oz) butter, melted and cooled
caster sugar, for dredging
6 tablespoons double cream
2 tablespoons dark rum (optional)
1 tablespoon icing sugar, sifted
CRÈME AU BEURRE AU CHOCOLAT:
75g (3oz) caster sugar
4 tablespoons water
2 egg yolks
100–175g (4–6oz) unsalted butter, beaten until soft
50g (2oz) plain chocolate, broken into pieces
1 tablespoon rum
DECORATION:
sifted icing sugar
marzipan holly leaves and berries (optional)

Preparation time: about 45 minutes
Cooking time: 25–30 minutes
Oven: 190°C, 375°F, Gas Mark 5

1. Line a 30 × 25cm (12 × 10 inch) Swiss roll tin.
2. Whisk the eggs and caster sugar together until the mixture is very thick and pale and the whisk leaves a heavy trail when it is lifted out. (Place the bowl over a pan of hot water if not whisking with an electric beater.)
3. Sift the flour and cocoa powder together twice and fold into the mixture, followed by the cooled but liquid butter.
4. Turn the mixture into the prepared tin. Place in a preheated oven and bake for 15–20 minutes, or until just firm and springy.
5. Turn out on to a piece of greaseproof paper dredged with caster sugar. Trim off the edges and quickly roll up the cake, with the paper inside. Allow to cool.
6. Whip the cream with the rum (if used) until stiff and then stir in the icing sugar. Unroll the cake carefully, remove the paper and spread evenly with the rum cream. Reroll carefully.
7. For the crème au beurre: gently dissolve the sugar in a heavy-based pan with the water. Boil steadily for 3–4 minutes or until 110°C (225°F) is reached on a sugar thermometer.

8. Pour the syrup in a thin stream on to the egg yolks, whisking constantly until thick and cold. Gradually beat into the butter.
9. Place the chocolate with the rum in a bowl over a pan of hot water and stir until smooth and melted. Cool, then beat into the crème au beurre.
10. Coat the cake with the crème au beurre, then mark attractively with a fork. Chill until set. Before serving, dredge the cake lightly with icing sugar and decorate with holly leaves and berries, if liked.

SERVES 8
Nutrition content per serving   Carbohydrate: 36g   Fat: 29g
Fibre: trace   Kilocalories: 439

YORKSHIRE JAM CAKE

350g (12oz) plain flour
pinch of salt
1 tablespoon baking powder
175g (6oz) butter or margarine
175g (6oz) caster sugar
1 egg (size 1 or 2), lightly beaten
50g (2oz) jam, warmed
GLAZE:
milk
caster sugar

Preparation time: 30 minutes
Cooking time: 30–35 minutes
Oven: 190°C, 375°F, Gas Mark 5

1. Sift the flour, salt and baking powder into a mixing bowl. Cut the fat into the flour and rub in with the fingertips until the mixture resembles breadcrumbs. Mix in the sugar thoroughly. Stir in the egg with a palette knife. Mix to a soft but not sticky dough, adding a little water if necessary.
2. Shape the dough into a ball and cut in half. On a floured board, roll each half out into a round 1cm (½ inch) thick.
3. Place one round on a greased baking sheet, prick it all over and spread with the warm jam, leaving a narrow margin around the edge. Cover with the second dough round and pinch the edges firmly together. Brush the top with milk and sprinkle with sugar. Mark into sections.
4. Bake in the centre of a preheated oven for 30–35 minutes, until well risen and golden brown. Cut through the marked lines with a sharp knife, then cool on a wire tray.

SERVES 6
Nutrition content per serving   Carbohydrate: 82g   Fat: 26g
Fibre: 2g   Kilocalories: 572

Yule log; Yorkshire jam cake

9. Warm the redcurrant jelly and brush over the strawberries.
10. Place the remaining cream in a piping bag fitted with a star tube. Pipe rosettes around the top edge of the cake.

Variation: When strawberries are not available or too expensive, try this gâteau with any other colourful fruit in season. Blackberries, peach slices, dessert plums, halved, or kiwi fruit slices are all suitable. To glaze the lighter coloured fruits, replace the redcurrant jelly with warmed, sieved apricot jam.

MAKES A 20CM (8 INCH) SANDWICH CAKE (8 SLICES)
Nutrition content per serving   Carbohydrate: 23g   Fat: 23g
Fibre: 1g   Kilocalories: 315

STRAWBERRY CREAM GÂTEAU

3 eggs
75g (3oz) caster sugar
75g (3oz) plain flour
25g (1oz) butter, melted
FILLING AND DECORATION:
300ml (½ pint) double or whipping cream
350g (12oz) strawberries
2 tablespoons redcurrant jelly

Preparation time: 20 minutes
Cooking time: 20–25 minutes
Oven: 180°C, 350°F, Gas Mark 4

1. Grease and line two 20cm (8 inch) sandwich tins.
2. Whisk the eggs and sugar together until thick and pale and the whisk leaves a trail when it is lifted out. (Place the bowl over a pan of hot water if not whisking with an electric beater.)
3. Sift the flour into the bowl and fold in lightly, using a metal spoon, until evenly mixed. Pour the melted butter slowly into the mixture and fold in.
4. Pour the mixture into the prepared tins. Shake the tins to level the mixture. Bake in a preheated oven for 20–25 minutes, until the cakes are golden brown and firm to the touch.
5. Turn out and cool on a wire tray.
6. Whip the cream until stiff. Slice half the strawberries.
7. Spread one-third of the cream over one cake and cover with the sliced strawberries. Place the second cake on top.
8. Spread half the remaining cream over the top of the cake. Cut the remaining strawberries in half and place on the top of the cake to within 2.5cm (1 inch) of the edge.

NUT TORTE

This continental torte is made like a whisked sponge but with ground nuts instead of flour and has a crisp caramel topping instead of icing. You can use walnuts, almonds, hazel or cashew nuts or a mixture of two or more kinds.

50g (2oz) unblanched almonds
50g (2oz) shelled walnuts
4 eggs, separated
150g (5oz) caster sugar
MOCHA BUTTERCREAM:
50g (2oz) unsalted butter, at room temperature
75g (3oz) icing sugar
1 teaspoon instant coffee powder
1½ teaspoons cocoa powder
CARAMEL TOPPING:
75g (3oz) sugar
3 tablespoons water
25g (1oz) walnut halves

Preparation time: 1 hour, plus cooling
Cooking time: 30 minutes
Oven: 180°C, 350°F, Gas Mark 4

1. Grease and line the bottoms of two 18cm (7 inch) sandwich tins.
2. Mince the nuts in a mouli grater or electric grinder.

Above: Strawberry cream gâteau
Opposite: Nut torte

Whisk together the egg yolks and caster sugar until a pale lemon colour. Whisk the whites until stiff but not too dry. Fold the whites and nuts into the egg yolks and sugar until well blended, but do not overfold.

3. Pour into the sandwich tins and level off. Bake on the same shelf in the centre of a preheated oven for 30 minutes or until set and the top springs back when gently pressed.

4. Remove from the oven and allow to shrink slightly before turning out on to a wire tray to cool.

5. For the buttercream, cream the butter until fluffy. Sift the sugar with the coffee and cocoa powders and beat gradually into the butter.

6. Put one of the cakes on a large serving plate, spread with buttercream and put the other cake on top.

7. Oil the edge of the plate so any drips of caramel can be easily removed. For the caramel, dissolve the sugar in the water in a small saucepan over a low heat. Stir until the syrup is clear, but do not allow to boil. When clear, raise the heat and boil rapidly without stirring until a rich caramel colour. Use immediately or the caramel will burn and turn too dark and make the torte bitter.

8. Pour the caramel on top of the torte, spreading it with an oiled palette knife neatly to the edge. Arrange the walnuts on top quickly before the caramel gets hard. Press the back of a knife into the caramel, marking it into 8 portions to make it easier to cut when serving. When the remaining caramel in the pan has cooled slightly, dip the end of the knife in it and draw it up in threads; trickle them over the nuts, or pull into spun sugar.

MAKES AN 18CM (7 INCH) SANDWICH CAKE (8 SLICES)
*Nutrition content per serving   Carbohydrate: 40g   Fat: 12g
Fibre: 1g   Kilocalories: 279*

PRALINE MERINGUE LAYER

The meringue and praline can both be made several days in advance if stored in airtight containers. Simply assemble when required.

4 egg whites
225g (8oz) caster sugar
PRALINE FILLING AND DECORATION:
75g (3oz) caster sugar
75g (3oz) whole unblanched almonds
450ml (¾ pint) double or whipping cream
ripe strawberries, raspberries, cherries or apricots

Preparation time: about 25 minutes, plus chilling
Cooking time: 2½–3 hours
Oven: 110°C, 225°F, Gas Mark ¼

1. Draw a rectangle 30 × 10cm (12 × 4 inches) on each of three sheets of non-stick silicone paper. Place on three baking sheets.
2. Whisk the egg whites until very stiff, then gradually whisk in the sugar a spoonful at a time, making sure the meringue is stiff again before adding further sugar.
3. Put the meringue into a piping bag fitted with a large star nozzle and pipe to cover the rectangles drawn on the paper.
4. Bake in a preheated oven for 2½–3 hours, moving the meringues around in the oven after each hour, until dry and crisp and easy to peel off the paper. Leave to cool.
5. Meanwhile, make the praline for the filling. Put the sugar and almonds into a small heavy-based saucepan and heat gently until the sugar melts. Shake the saucepan to coat all the nuts with the sugar syrup, but do not stir. Cook gently until the sugar turns a good caramel colour, shaking the pan from time to time.
6. Spoon four individual almonds on to one end of a well-greased sheet, making sure they are evenly coated in caramel. Quickly pour the remaining praline mixture on to the other end of the sheet and leave until cold.
7. Reserving the four individual almonds, crush the sheet of praline using a rolling pin, pestle and mortar, small mouli cheese grater, liquidizer or food processor (but take care as it may well scratch the surface of the bowl).
8. Assemble the gâteau not more than 45 minutes before required. Whip the cream until stiff; put about one-third of it into a piping bag fitted with a large star nozzle. Fold the crushed praline into the remaining cream.
9. Place one meringue layer on a plate or board, spread with half the praline cream and cover with the second meringue layer. Spread over the rest of the praline cream and top with the third meringue layer.
10. Pipe whirls or a zig-zag pattern of cream along the top of the gâteau and decorate with the whole caramelled almonds and fresh fruit. Chill for 10–15 minutes before serving.

SERVES 8
Nutrition content per serving   Carbohydrate: 43g   Fat: 32g
Fibre: 2g   Kilocalories: 464

DANISH APPLE TORTE

750g (1½lb) cooking apples, peeled and cored
grated rind and juice of 1 lemon
50g (2oz) granulated sugar
5 tablespoons sweet or medium sherry
28 ginger biscuits
DECORATION:
300ml (½ pint) whipping or double cream
25g (1oz) plain chocolate

Preparation time: about 30 minutes, plus chilling
Cooking time: 20–25 minutes

1. Slice the apples into a saucepan, then add the lemon rind and lemon juice. Cover and simmer gently for 10–15 minutes until tender.
2. Remove the lid. Add the sugar and simmer for 10 minutes, stirring occasionally, until a thick purée is formed. Remove from the heat; leave until cold.
3. Pour the sherry into a small bowl. Dip in one biscuit and place it in the centre of a large flat plate. Dip in six more biscuits and arrange in a circle round the first one, all touching.
4. Spread one-third of the apple purée over the biscuits, keeping within the curved outline.
5. Repeat the biscuit and apple layers, first dipping the biscuits into the sherry, and finishing with a layer of biscuits. Remove any purée from the sides of the gâteau and chill until set.
6. Whip the cream until stiff and cover the gâteau completely.
7. Melt the chocolate in a heatproof bowl over a pan of hot water. Put into a small paper piping bag. Cut off the tip of the bag and pipe lines across the top of the gâteau. Eat the same day.

SERVES 8
Nutrition content per serving   Carbohydrate: 44g   Fat: 24g
Fibre: 3g   Kilocalories: 399

Praline meringue layer; Danish apple torte

BELGIAN TORTE

225g (8oz) butter, at room temperature
75g (3oz) caster sugar
2 tablespoons oil
¼ teaspoon vanilla essence
1 egg (size 1 or 2), beaten
450g (1lb) plain flour
2 teaspoons baking powder
225g (8oz) apricot jam
75g (3oz) dried apricots, finely chopped
TOPPING:
1 × 425g (15oz) can apricot halves
1 tablespoon sherry
a little icing sugar

Preparation time: 25 minutes
Cooking time: 1¾ hours
Oven: 150°C, 300°F, Gas Mark 2

1. Grease a 20cm (8 inch) cake tin with a removable base, or line the bottom of an ordinary cake tin with non-stick silicone paper or greased greaseproof paper.
2. Cream the butter and sugar together until light and fluffy, then beat in the oil. Add the vanilla essence and beaten egg and beat well.
3. Sift the flour with the baking powder and gradually work into the creamed mixture. Knead the mixture together as for a shortbread dough.
4. Divide the dough in half and coarsely grate one portion into the tin to cover the bottom evenly.
5. Beat the jam until smooth and spread lightly over the dough layer, taking it almost to the edges. Sprinkle with the dried apricots.
6. Grate the remaining dough evenly over the jam.
7. Place in a preheated oven just above the centre and bake for 1½ hours, until lightly browned. Remove from the oven and leave until cool, loosening the torte from the sides of the tin with a palette knife as it cools.
8. Drain the canned apricots and boil the syrup with the sherry until reduced to about 3 tablespoons; cool slightly.
9. Remove the torte carefully from the tin and slide on to a serving plate. Arrange the apricot halves around the edge of the torte and brush a little syrup over each, allowing it to run down the sides. Sprinkle sifted icing sugar in the centre and serve.

MAKES A 20CM (8 INCH) ROUND CAKE (8 SLICES)
Nutrition content per serving   Carbohydrate: 92g   Fat: 28g
Fibre: 5g   Kilocalories: 627

CHOCOLATE GÂTEAU

100g (4oz) butter, at room temperature
175g (6oz) caster sugar
175g (6oz) plain chocolate
75g (3oz) plain flour
1 teaspoon baking powder
6 eggs, separated
FILLING:
225g (8oz) plain chocolate
250ml (8floz) double cream
2 tablespoons brandy
DECORATION:
chocolate scrolls
icing sugar

Preparation time: 30 minutes
Cooking time: 1 hour
Oven: 180°C, 350°F, Gas Mark 4

1. Grease and flour a 20cm (8 inch) round cake tin with a removable base.
2. Cream the butter and the sugar together until light and fluffy.
3. Melt the chocolate in a bowl set over a pan of hot water.
4. Add the melted chocolate to the creamed butter.
5. Sift the flour and baking powder together. Add the egg yolks to the creamed mixture one by one, incorporating a little flour mixture each time and beat together well. Stir in the rest of the flour.
6. Whisk the egg whites until they stand in soft peaks.
7. Fold the egg whites gently into the chocolate mixture. (It is easiest to do this using your hand.)
8. Pour the mixture into the prepared tin and bake in a preheated oven for 1 hour, until the surface is firm.
9. Leave the cake to cool in the tin for a few minutes before turning it out on to a wire tray to cool completely.
10. Meanwhile, prepare the filling. Melt the chocolate in a bowl set over a pan of hot water and stir in the cream and brandy. Leave to cool and thicken.
11. When cool, whip the mixture until it becomes lighter in texture and increases in volume.
12. Slice the cake horizontally into three layers and sandwich each layer with a little chocolate cream.
13. Set the bowl of remaining chocolate cream over the pan of hot water to melt it down again, if necessary, then pour the chocolate cream over the cake. Decorate with chocolate scrolls and dust lightly with the icing sugar.

MAKES A 20CM (8 INCH) THREE-LAYER CAKE (8 SLICES)
Nutrition content per serving   Carbohydrate: 64g   Fat: 45g
Fibre: trace   Kilocalories: 688

Chocolate gâteau (top); Belgian torte

APRICOT CHEESECAKE

SOURED CREAM PASTRY:
150g (5oz) plain flour, sifted
100g (4oz) butter
1 tablespoon caster sugar
1 egg yolk
1 tablespoon soured cream
FILLING:
2 tablespoons ground almonds
450g (1lb) fresh apricots, halved and stoned, or
750g (1½lb) canned apricots, well drained,
syrup reserved
1½ teaspoons ground cinnamon
50g (2oz) granulated sugar (if using fresh apricots)
50g (2oz) butter, at room temperature
2 egg yolks
185g (6½oz) curd cheese
50g (2oz) caster sugar
½ teaspoon grated lemon rind
1 tablespoon double cream
DECORATION:
1 teaspoon arrowroot
whipped cream
flaked toasted almonds

Preparation time: 45 minutes plus chilling and cooling
Cooking time: 1 hour 10 minutes
Oven: 180°C, 350°F, Gas Mark 4

1. For the pastry, sift the flour into a bowl. Cut in the butter and lightly rub in with the fingertips until the mixture resembles breadcrumbs. Mix in the sugar. Add the egg yolk and soured cream and blend to a smooth pliable pastry. Roll into a ball, cover with cling film and chill for 1 hour.
2. Roll out the pastry and line a greased 22cm (8½ inch) springform tin, pushing the pastry 2.5cm (1 inch) up the sides. Scatter the ground almonds over the bottom of the pastry case.

3. Reserve 4 apricot halves for decoration. Pack the rest into the pastry case. Mix together 1 teaspoon of cinnamon and the granulated sugar and sprinkle over the apricots (if using canned fruit omit the sugar).
4. Beat the butter with the egg yolks until light and creamy. Mix in the curd cheese, caster sugar, lemon rind, double cream and remaining cinnamon.
5. Pour the mixture on to the fruit in the tin and bake in a preheated oven for 1 hour 10 minutes. Cool in the tin on a wire tray.
6. Carefully remove the sides of the tin and set the cheesecake on a serving plate. Slice the reserved apricot halves and arrange them on top. If available, mix 120ml (4floz) of the reserved apricot syrup with the arrowroot and stir over a low heat until thickened. Glaze the apricots, then cool. Decorate with whipped cream and flaked almonds and serve.

MAKES A 22CM (8½ INCH) CHEESECAKE (8 SLICES)
Nutrition content per serving   Carbohydrate: 46g   Fat: 23g
Fibre: 2g   Kilocalories: 405

HAZELNUT DREAM CAKE

90g (3½oz) plain flour
15g (½oz) cornflour
2 teaspoons instant coffee powder
4 eggs
100g (4oz) caster sugar
40g (1½oz) butter, melted
40–50g (1½–2oz) toasted hazelnuts, finely chopped or ground
24 toasted hazelnuts, to decorate
CRÈME PÂTISSIÈRE:
300ml (½ pint) milk
50g (2oz) caster sugar
20g (¾oz) plain flour
15g (½oz) cornflour
1 egg, plus 1 egg yolk
a few drops of vanilla essence
15g (½oz) butter
GLACÉ ICING:
100g (4oz) icing sugar, sifted
2–3 teaspoons coffee essence

Preparation time: 45 minutes
Cooking time: about 20 minutes
Oven: 190°C, 375°F, Gas Mark 5

1. Grease and line a 33 × 23cm (13 × 9 inch) tin.
2. Sift the flour, cornflour and instant coffee powder twice.

3. Whisk the eggs and sugar together until very thick and pale and the whisk leaves a trail when it is lifted out. (Place the bowl over a pan of hot water if not whisking with an electric beater.)

4. Fold in most of the sifted flour, then add the cooled, but still liquid, butter, and finally the remaining flour, folding lightly.

5. Turn into the prepared tin, making sure there is plenty of mixture in the corners. Place in a preheated oven and bake for about 20 minutes or until well risen and just firm to the touch. Turn out on to a wire tray and leave to cool.

6. For the crème pâtissière: gently heat the milk. Beat the sugar, flour, cornflour, egg and yolk together until smooth. Beat in a little of the warmed milk, return it all to the pan and bring to the boil, stirring continuously, until thickened. Cook gently for about 1 minute. Remove from the heat and stir in the vanilla essence and butter. Cover with a piece of wet greaseproof paper or cling film and leave until cold.

7. Strip the paper off the cake and cut across into 3 even-sized layers. Beat the chopped hazelnuts into the cold crème pâtissière and use to sandwich the cakes together.

8. For the glacé icing: sift the sugar into a bowl and add the coffee essence and sufficient water to give a smooth icing that will coat the back of a spoon. Use to spread over the top of the cake.

9. Add clusters of 3 hazelnuts for decoration and leave to set.

MAKES A 23 × 10CM (9 × 4 INCH) THREE-LAYER CAKE
(10 SLICES)
*Nutrition content per serving   Carbohydrate: 40g   Fat: 10g
Fibre: trace   Kilocalories: 266*

*Below: Hazelnut dream cake
Opposite: Apricot cheesecake*

TIPSY ORANGE RING

100g (4oz) soft tub margarine
100g (4oz) caster sugar
2 eggs
100g (4oz) self-raising flour
1 teaspoon baking powder
2 teaspoons grated orange rind
SYRUP:
100g (4oz) granulated sugar
150ml (¼ pint) water
juice of 1 medium orange
2 tablespoons orange-flavoured liqueur or medium sherry
DECORATION:
2 medium oranges
100g (4oz) black grapes, halved and seeded
2 tablespoons apricot jam, boiled and sieved

Preparation time: 45 minutes, plus cooling and soaking
Cooking time: 35–40 minutes
Oven: 170°C, 325°F, Gas Mark 3

1. Grease a 20cm (8 inch) ring mould and line the bottom with greased greaseproof paper.
2. Put the margarine, sugar, eggs, sifted flour, baking powder and orange rind in a bowl and beat until smooth and glossy.
3. Put the mixture into the prepared mould and bake in a preheated oven for 35–40 minutes, until the cake will spring back when lightly pressed in the centre. Cool on a wire tray.
4. Put the sugar and water for the syrup in a saucepan and stir over a low heat until the sugar has dissolved. Bring to the boil and boil rapidly for 1 minute without stirring. Remove from the heat and cool. Add the orange juice and liqueur or sherry to the syrup.
5. Replace the cake in the ring mould in which it was baked and pour over the syrup. Leave in the mould until all the syrup has been absorbed, then invert the cake on to a serving plate.
6. Cut the peel and pith from the oranges with a sharp or serrated knife. Cut in between the membrane to remove the orange segments.
7. To decorate, arrange orange segments around the cake; arrange orange segments and halved grapes alternately around the centre hole of the cake ring and pile the remaining fruit in the centre. Brush the cake and fruit with apricot jam to glaze.

MAKES A 20CM (8 INCH) RING CAKE (8 SLICES)
Nutrition content per serving   Carbohydrate: 44g   Fat: 12g
Fibre: 1g   Kilocalories: 289

BLACK FOREST GÂTEAU

6 eggs
175g (6oz) caster sugar
175g (6oz) plain flour
50g (2oz) cocoa powder
120ml (4floz) kirsch or cherry brandy
2 × 450g (15oz) cans black cherries, drained, stoned and halved, juice reserved
FILLING:
600ml (1 pint) double cream, whipped
2 teaspoons arrowroot
75g (3oz) plain dark chocolate, grated, or chocolate scrolls, to decorate

Preparation time: 50 minutes, plus overnight soaking
Cooking time: 30–40 minutes
Oven: 190°C, 375°F, Gas Mark 5

1. Grease and flour two 20cm (8 inch) round cake tins.
2. Whisk the eggs and sugar together until pale and thick and the whisk leaves a trail when it is lifted out. (Place the bowl over a pan of hot water if not whisking with an electric beater.)
3. Sift in the flour and cocoa powder and fold them gently into the egg mixture.
4. Divide the mixture between the prepared tins and bake in a preheated oven for 30–40 minutes or until firm and spongy.
5. Leave the cakes to cool slightly in the tins, then turn them out on to wire trays. When they are cold, split each cake in half horizontally.
6. Sprinkle 2 tablespoons of kirsch and 4 tablespoons of cherry juice on each layer. Soak overnight.
7. Sandwich a third of the cream and half the black cherries between each layer of chocolate cake.
8. Spread half the remaining cream around the sides of the cake. Arrange the remaining cherries in concentric circles on top of the cake, leaving a border for rosettes of whipped cream.
9. Slake the arrowroot with a little water and stir it into 150ml (¼ pint) cherry juice. Bring the juice gently to the boil, stirring continuously until it clears and thickens. Pour the cherry sauce over the cherries on top of the cake.
10. Pipe a border of cream rosettes round the edge of the cake and cover the sides of the cake with grated chocolate or chocolate scrolls.

MAKES A 20CM (8 INCH) FOUR-LAYER CAKE (10 SLICES)
Nutrition content per serving   Carbohydrate: 58g   Fat: 32g
Fibre: 1g   Kilocalories: 556

Tipsy orange ring; Black Forest gâteau

PIES & TARTS

*There's nothing like the taste and texture of good pastry –
crisp and crumbly puff and rough puff, tender, melting
in the mouth shortcrust, and light-as-air choux. The
fillings for the flans, tarts, pies and puffs in this chapter
are simply irresistible: fresh fruits, rich custards,
chocolate cream, whipped cream, almond paste, curd
cheese and jam, sweet nuts in a syrup mixture, and dried
fruits such as raisins and dates.*

RED FRUIT BAGATELLE

350g (12oz) puff pastry, thawed if frozen
beaten egg, to glaze
1 recipe quantity crème pâtissière (see Hazelnut
Dream Cake, page 42)
1–2 tablespoons brandy or orange liqueur
FILLING:
1 × 425g (15oz) can black cherries, stoned if necessary
2 firm pears
2 teaspoons arrowroot
100g (4oz) strawberries
100g (4oz) raspberries, fresh or frozen and thawed

Preparation time: about 1 hour, plus chilling
Cooking time: about 25 minutes
Oven: 220°C, 425°F, Gas Mark 7

1. Roll out the pastry on a floured surface to an oblong 8–10mm (⅓–½ inch) thick and trim to about 30 × 15cm (12 × 6 inches).
2. Fold in half lengthways and cut out a rectangle, cutting across the fold and leaving 3 edges as a border about 2.5cm (1 inch) wide. Unfold. Roll out the cut out rectangle of pastry to the same size as the 'frame'; place on a lightly greased baking sheet.
3. Brush the edges of the rectangle with beaten egg and position the 'frame' on top, pressing firmly together. Knock up the sides and mark a lattice pattern on the pastry border with the back of a knife. Brush with beaten egg to glaze, prick the base of the tart and chill for 10 minutes.
4. Place in a preheated oven and bake for about 20 minutes or until well risen and golden brown. Cool slightly and then remove carefully to a wire tray and leave until cold.
5. Make up the crème pâtissière, beat in the brandy or liqueur, cover with cling film and leave until cold.
6. Drain the cherries and put the juice into a saucepan. Peel, core and slice the pears and poach in the cherry juice for about 5 minutes or until just tender. Drain the pears and mix with the cherries. Leave about 225ml (8floz) cherry juice in the saucepan. Blend the arrowroot with a little cold water, add to the juice and bring to the boil, stirring until thickened and clear. Cool.
7. To assemble: put the pastry case on a serving dish or board and spread the crème pâtissière inside.
8. Arrange the cherries with the slices of pear, halved or sliced strawberries and raspberries in the pastry case over the custard. Spoon over the cherry juice glaze and chill for about 1 hour before serving.

SERVES 10
Nutrition content per serving   Carbohydrate: 38g   Fat: 12g
Fibre: 3g   Kilocalories: 276

CARIBBEAN FLAN

1½ recipe quantities shortcrust pastry (see Gooseberry
& Orange Plate Pie, page 57)
50g (2oz) plain flour
½ teaspoon baking powder
50g (2oz) caster sugar
50g (2oz) soft tub margarine or softened butter
1 egg
25g (1oz) fine desiccated coconut
grated rind of 2 oranges
TOPPING:
3 bananas
40g (1½oz) butter
50g (2oz) demerara sugar
150ml (¼ pint) orange juice
juice of ½ lemon

Preparation time: 25 minutes
Cooking time: 30 minutes
Oven: 190°C, 375°F, Gas Mark 5

1. Roll out the pastry and use to line a 22cm (8½ inch) flan ring placed on a baking sheet.
2. Sift the flour, baking powder and sugar into a bowl. Add the margarine or butter, egg, desiccated coconut and orange rind. Beat the ingredients together until the mixture is light and fluffy.
3. Fill the pastry case with the sponge mixture. Place in a preheated oven and bake for about 30 minutes, until a light golden brown. Remove from the flan ring.
4. Cut the bananas into 5mm (¼ inch) thick slices. Heat the butter in a frying pan, toss the bananas in the demerara sugar and fry quickly over a moderate heat until lightly coloured on both sides. Arrange closely in circles on top of the sponge.
5. Pour the orange and lemon juices into the frying pan and boil until 3–4 tablespoons remain. Pour over the bananas and serve, hot or cold.

SERVES 8
Nutrition content per serving   Carbohydrate: 44g   Fat: 21g
Fibre: 3g   Kilocalories: 376

Red fruit bagatelle (top); Caribbean flan

GLAZED LEMON FLAN

In this recipe, the soft sharp filling contrasts well with the crisp, sweet pastry base.

175g (6oz) plain flour
pinch of salt
75g (3oz) caster sugar
75g (3oz) butter, at room temperature
3 egg yolks
FILLING:
3 eggs
175g (6oz) caster sugar
grated rind and juice of 3 thin-skinned lemons
50g (2oz) butter, melted
DECORATION:
50g (2oz) sugar
300ml (½ pint) water
1 thin-skinned lemon, sliced

Preparation time: 30 minutes
Cooking time: 45 minutes
Oven: 190°C, 375°F, Gas Mark 5

1. For the pastry, sift the flour and salt into a bowl. Stir in the caster sugar. Make a well in the centre and add the butter and egg yolks. Work together to give a firm dough. Roll out on a lightly floured surface and use to line a 24cm (9½ inch) fluted flan tin. Chill.
2. Beat together the ingredients for the filling. Set aside.
3. For the decoration, dissolve the sugar in the water. Bring to the boil and boil for 2 minutes. Add the lemon slices and continue to boil gently until the syrup has almost disappeared, taking care that the lemon slices stay whole. Leave on a plate to cool. Reserve the remaining syrup.
4. Bake the pastry case blind in a preheated oven for 15 minutes. Pour in the filling and return to the oven to bake for a further 20–25 minutes, until the filling is just set.
5. Allow to cool slightly, then decorate with lemon slices, arranged around the edge of the flan. Glaze the lemon slices with the reserved syrup. Leave until cold.

SERVES 8
Nutrition content per serving   Carbohydrate: 57g   Fat: 15g
Fibre: 1g   Kilocalories: 364

CRACKLING PIE

175g (6oz) ground almonds
50g (2oz) caster sugar
1 teaspoon rum
1 egg white, beaten
FILLING:
250ml (8floz) double cream
225g (8oz) plain chocolate, broken into pieces
1 egg yolk
1 tablespoon icing sugar
1 tablespoon rum
TOPPING:
4 egg whites
100g (4oz) caster sugar
25g (1oz) flaked almonds

Preparation time: 30 minutes, plus cooling
Cooking time: 40–50 minutes
Oven: 180°C, 350°F, Gas Mark 4; then
230°C, 450°F, Gas Mark 8

1. Butter a 20cm (8 inch) flan ring placed on a baking sheet.
2. Combine the almonds, sugar, rum and beaten egg white, and work to a stiff paste. Shape into a ball, wrap and chill for 30 minutes.
3. Roll out the paste on a lightly floured surface and use to line the ring. If the paste breaks, gently press it into the ring. Line the inside edge of the shell with a strip of foil and bake in a preheated oven for 20–25 minutes or until lightly browned. Remove to a wire tray and leave until cool before carefully removing the foil and flan ring.
4. To prepare the filling, place the cream and chocolate pieces in a saucepan over a low heat. Stir constantly until the chocolate melts and the mixture is thick and smooth. Remove from the heat and leave to cool slightly.
5. Stir in the egg yolk. Add the icing sugar and rum and beat until light and fluffy. Fill the almond shell with the chocolate mixture.
6. For the topping, whisk the egg whites until stiff, then gradually whisk in the sugar until firm and glossy. Spread the meringue over the chocolate, slightly overlapping the shell. Scatter the flaked almonds over the top.
7. Bake in a preheated oven at the higher temperature for 5 minutes or until the meringue is lightly browned.

SERVES 6
Nutrition content per serving   Carbohydrate: 55g   Fat: 50g
Fibre: 5g   Kilocalories: 708

Glazed lemon flan; Crackling pie

PEACH CREAM FLAN

RICH SWEET SHORTCRUST PASTRY:
100g (4oz) plain flour
50g (2oz) butter or margarine
15g (½oz) lard
2 teaspoons caster sugar
1 egg yolk
FILLING:
250ml (8floz) milk
50–65g (2–2½oz) caster sugar
1½ tablespoons cornflour
few drops of almond essence
2 egg yolks
1 × 425g (15oz) can peach slices, drained
DECORATION:
whipping cream
pistachio nuts or strips of candied angelica

Preparation time: 40 minutes, plus cooling
Cooking time: about 20 minutes
Oven: 200°C, 400°F, Gas Mark 6

1. Sift the flour into a bowl and rub in the fats until the mixture resembles breadcrumbs. Mix together the sugar and egg yolk and add to the flour mixture with a little iced water if necessary to mix to a soft, not sticky dough.
2. Roll out the dough and use to line a 20cm (8 inch) flan ring or dish. Bake blind in a preheated oven for 20 minutes or until set and golden brown. Cool on a wire tray.
3. To make the filling, put the milk, sugar and cornflour in a small saucepan and bring to the boil, stirring continuously. Boil for 1 minute, then beat in the almond essence and egg yolks. Cook gently for a further minute, then pour into the flan case and leave to cool.
4. Arrange the peach slices over the custard filling. Decorate around the peaches with stars or swirls of whipped cream and top with chopped pistachio nuts or pieces of angelica.

SERVES 6
Nutrition content per serving   Carbohydrate: 46g   Fat: 14g
Fibre: 1g   Kilocalories: 318

STRAWBERRY CHOUX RING

If the choux dough is piped in swirls on the baking sheet, the finished effect of this dessert will be really quite spectacular.

150g (5oz) plain flour
¼ teaspoon salt
300ml (½ pint) water
100g (4oz) butter or margarine
4 eggs, beaten
FILLING:
300ml (½ pint) double cream
50g (2oz) icing sugar, sifted
450g (1lb) fresh strawberries, hulled
about 2 tablespoons caster sugar

Preparation time: 45 minutes, plus cooling
Cooking time: 40–45 minutes
Oven: 200°C, 400°F, Gas Mark 6

1. To make the choux pastry, sift the flour and salt on to a sheet of greaseproof paper. Put the water in a pan with the butter or margarine and heat gently until the fat has melted. Bring to the boil and, when bubbling vigorously, remove from the heat and immediately add the flour all at once. Beat well with a wooden spoon until the mixture forms a ball and draws away from the sides of the pan.
2. Leave the mixture to cool until lukewarm, then beat in the eggs, a little at a time, until the pastry is smooth and glossy and has a piping consistency.
3. Put the choux paste in a piping bag fitted with a large plain nozzle and pipe a 23cm (9 inch) ring on a greased large baking sheet.
4. Bake just above the centre of the oven for 40–45 minutes, until the pastry is well risen and golden brown. Transfer to a wire tray and leave to cool.
5. Meanwhile, make the filling: whip the cream and icing sugar until thick. Chop about half the strawberries roughly and fold into the cream.
6. Cut the choux ring into 6 equal portions, then slice each portion in half. Divide the strawberry cream mixture equally between each portion, then sandwich the halves together again. Re-assemble the choux ring on a serving plate, then pile the remaining whole strawberries in the centre.
7. Just before serving, sprinkle the strawberries with caster sugar to taste. Serve as soon as possible.

SERVES 6
Nutrition content per serving   Carbohydrate: 39g   Fat: 41g
Fibre: 3g   Kilocalories: 545

Strawberry choux ring (top); Peach cream flan

GÂTEAU PITHIVIERS

100g (4oz) unsalted butter, at room temperature
100g (4oz) caster sugar
1 egg, beaten with 1 egg yolk
100g (4oz) ground almonds
2 tablespoons rum
400g (14oz) puff pastry, thawed if frozen
GLAZE:
1 egg, beaten
a little icing sugar

Preparation time: 45 minutes
Cooking time: 30–35 minutes
Oven: 220°C, 425°F, Gas Mark 7

1. Cream the butter and sugar together until light and fluffy. Beat in the egg and egg yolk mixture, then beat in the almonds and rum until evenly mixed. Set aside.

2. Roll out half the pastry on a floured surface to a 23cm (9 inch) round. Place the round on a dampened baking sheet. Spread the filling over the pastry to within about 1cm (½ inch) of the edge, mounding it up in the centre. Brush the exposed edge of the pastry with water.

3. Roll out the remaining pastry to a 25cm (10 inch) round. Cut away a narrow strip all round the edge of this round. Press this strip around the moistened edge of the round on the baking sheet. Brush the strip with water. Cover the filling with the second round of pastry, pressing it down firmly at the edge to seal. Knock up the edge with the back of a knife, then give the edge a scalloped effect by pressing your thumb around it at regular intervals and marking in between each thumb mark with the back of the knife.

4. Make a hole in the centre of the gâteau with a skewer, and brush all over the pastry with the beaten egg, taking care not to brush the decorated edge or the pastry will not rise. With a sharp knife, make shallow semi-circular cuts in the pastry all round the top of the gâteau, working from the centre towards the outside edge.

5. Bake in a preheated oven for 25–30 minutes, until puffed up and golden brown. Sift the icing sugar evenly over the top of the gâteau and return to the oven to bake for a further 5 minutes until glazed and shiny.

6. Leave to stand on the baking sheet for a few minutes, then carefully transfer to a wire tray. Serve warm or cold, with cream.

SERVES 6
Nutrition content per serving   Carbohydrate: 43g   Fat: 41g
Fibre: 4g   Kilocalories: 583

SPICED BRAMBLE PIE

300g (11oz) blackberries, hulled
200g (7oz) cooking apples, peeled, cored and thinly sliced
juice of ½ lemon
½ teaspoon ground ginger
¼ teaspoon ground mace
½ teaspoon mixed spice
75g (3oz) soft brown sugar
300g (11oz) puff pastry, thawed if frozen
1 egg yolk

Preparation time: 20 minutes
Cooking time: 45 minutes
Oven: 240°C, 475°F, Gas Mark 9; then
190°C, 375°F, Gas Mark 5

1. Mix all the ingredients together except for the puff pastry and egg yolk. Transfer to a 900ml (1½ pint) pie dish.

2. Roll out the pastry into an oval shape roughly 5cm (2 inches) wider than the pie dish.

3. Cut a 2.5cm (1 inch) strip from the circumference of the rolled pastry and use to cover the entire rim of the pie dish. Trim.

4. Brush the rim with water, then cover with the lid of pastry. Trim the edges with kitchen scissors or a very sharp knife.

5. Press the edges together and flute the pastry. Make a hole in the centre of the pie to let the steam escape during cooking.

6. Decorate the top with trimmings cut into leaf shapes. Brush with the egg yolk.

7. Bake for 20 minutes in a preheated oven. Reduce the heat and bake for a further 25 minutes.

SERVES 6
Nutrition content per serving   Carbohydrate: 37g   Fat: 13g
Fibre: 6g   Kilocalories: 272

Gâteau Pithiviers (top); Spiced bramble pie

bake in a preheated oven for 15 minutes, until the pastry is golden brown.

5. Beat together the remaining sugar, the egg and flour until smooth. Beat in the milk and brandy (if using), until evenly mixed.

6. Pour the custard over the pears in the pastry case. Reduce the oven temperature and return the tart to the oven to bake for a further 20 minutes, until the filling is set. Serve warm or cold.

SERVES 8
*Nutrition content per serving   Carbohydrate: 37g   Fat: 11g
Fibre: 3g   Kilocalories: 273*

CURD CHEESE JAM TART

This must be eaten the day it is made.

250g (9oz) curd cheese
250g (9oz) plain flour, sifted
100g (4oz) butter, softened
1 tablespoon caster sugar
pinch of salt
1 egg
250g (8oz) plum, gooseberry or damson jam

*Preparation time: 35 minutes
Cooking time: 40 minutes
Oven: 180°C, 350°F, Gas Mark 4*

1. Mix together the cheese and flour. Blend in the butter, sugar and salt. Mix in the egg and knead to a smooth dough.

2. Roll out two-thirds of the dough on a floured surface to a thickness of 1cm (½ inch). Use to line a greased 26cm (10½ inch) fluted flan ring. Spread the jam thickly in the pastry case.

3. Roll out the rest of the pastry to the same thickness and cut into long strips 1 cm (½ inch) wide. Lay them on top of the tart in a lattice pattern.

PEAR & HAZELNUT TART

PASTRY:
175g (6oz) plain flour
1 tablespoon caster sugar
75g (3oz) butter, diced
25g (1oz) ground hazelnuts
1 egg yolk
2 teaspoons iced water
FILLING:
2–3 medium pears
75g (3oz) caster sugar
1 egg
25g (1oz) plain flour
150ml (¼ pint) milk
3 tablespoons brandy (optional)

*Preparation time: 30 minutes
Cooking time: 35 minutes
Oven: 220°C, 425°F, Gas Mark 7; then
190°C, 375°F, Gas Mark 5*

1. To make the pastry, place the flour, sugar, butter, hazelnuts, egg yolk and water in a bowl. Work the ingredients together with the fingertips to form a firm dough.

2. Turn out on to a lightly floured surface and knead lightly. Roll out and line a 23cm (9 inch) flan tin.

3. To make the filling, peel, halve and core the pears, then with cut side down, slice thinly lengthways. Place in the flan case radiating from the centre.

4. Sprinkle the pears with 25g (1oz) of the sugar and

4. Bake in a preheated oven for 40 minutes, until golden.
5. Serve either warm or cold, with cream.

SERVES 8
Nutrition content per serving   Carbohydrate: 48g   Fat: 15g
Fibre: 1g   Kilocalories: 341

GOOSEBERRY & ORANGE PLATE PIE

450g (1lb) gooseberries, topped and tailed
grated rind of 1 orange
50–75g (2–3oz) caster sugar, to taste
2 oranges, peeled and segmented
a little extra caster sugar, to finish
SHORTCRUST PASTRY:
100g (4oz) plain flour
pinch of salt
25g (1oz) butter or margarine
25g (1oz) lard
about 1 tablespoon iced water

Preparation time: 20–30 minutes
Cooking time: 30–40 minutes
Oven: 200°C, 400°F, Gas Mark 6

1. To make the pastry, sift the flour and salt into a bowl. Cut in the fats, then rub in with the fingertips until the mixture resembles fine breadcrumbs. Mix in the water to bind to a soft, not sticky, dough.
2. Roll out two-thirds of the dough and line a 25cm (10 inch) pie plate.
3. Mix the gooseberries with the grated orange rind and sugar and place in the pastry case. Arrange the orange segments over the top.
4. Roll out the remainder of the dough. Moisten the edge of the pastry case and place the pastry 'lid' over the top of the fruit. Seal well and knock up and flute the edge.
5. Make a hole in the top of the pie to allow the steam to escape. Place on a hot baking sheet and bake in a preheated oven for 30–40 minutes, until golden brown.
6. Sprinkle a little caster sugar over the top of the pie and serve hot or warm.

SERVES 6
Nutrition content per serving   Carbohydrate: 36g   Fat: 8g
Fibre: 4g   Kilocalories: 216

Below: Gooseberry & orange plate pie
Opposite top: Pear & hazelnut tart
Opposite bottom: Curd cheese jam tart

LINZER TORTE

350g (12oz) frozen raspberries
225g (8oz) caster sugar
2 tablespoons arrowroot
2 tablespoons water
3–4 tablespoons redcurrant jelly, to glaze
PASTRY:
175g (6oz) plain flour
pinch of salt
pinch of ground cinnamon
65g (2½oz) ground almonds
65g (2½oz) caster sugar
50g (2oz) butter or margarine
1 egg, beaten

Preparation time: 1 hour, plus chilling
Cooking time: 35 minutes
Oven: 190°C, 375°F, Gas Mark 5

1. To make the filling: put the raspberries and sugar in a pan, reserving 10 whole raspberries for decoration. Heat gently until the raspberries have thawed and the sugar has dissolved. Bring to the boil, then lower the heat and cook for 10–15 minutes, until the consistency of thin jam, stirring frequently. Remove the pan from the heat.
2. Mix the arrowroot to a paste with the water, then stir gradually into the raspberry mixture. Return to the heat and bring back to the boil, then simmer until thick and clear, stirring constantly. Leave to cool.
3. Meanwhile, make the pastry: sift the flour, salt and cinnamon into a bowl, then stir in the almonds and sugar. Cut in the butter or margarine, then rub into the flour with the fingertips. Stir in the egg, then gather the dough together gently with the fingertips and form into a ball. Chill in the refrigerator for at least 30 minutes.
4. Reserve a small piece of dough for the lattice topping, then press the remaining dough into a 20cm (8 inch) plain flan ring placed on a baking sheet. Chill in the refrigerator for a further 15 minutes.
5. Spread the cooled raspberry mixture in the flan case. Roll out the reserved dough into strips and place across the filling in a lattice pattern, sealing the edges with water. Place the reserved whole raspberries in the 'windows' of the lattice.
6. Bake in a preheated oven for 35 minutes, then leave to cool on the baking sheet. Remove the flan ring carefully and transfer the tart to a serving plate. Melt the redcurrant jelly in a small pan, brush over the top of the tart and leave to cool. Serve cold, with whipped cream.

SERVES 6
Nutrition content per serving   Carbohydrate: 72g   Fat: 14g
Fibre: 7g   Kilocalories: 423

PECAN PIE

RICH SWEET SHORTCRUST PASTRY:
175g (6oz) plain flour
pinch of salt
100g (4oz) unsalted butter
25g (1oz) sugar
about 1 tablespoon iced water
FILLING:
100g (4oz) shelled pecan nuts
3 eggs
250ml (8floz) corn syrup or golden syrup
75g (3oz) light brown sugar
½ teaspoon vanilla essence
¼ teaspoon salt

Preparation time: 25 minutes
Cooking time: 40 minutes
Oven: 220°C, 425°F, Gas Mark 7; then
180°C, 350°F, Gas Mark 4

1. Sift the flour and salt into a bowl. Rub in the butter with the fingertips until the mixture resembles breadcrumbs, then add the sugar and mix with enough water to make a firm dough.
2. Roll out on a lightly floured surface and use to line a 24cm (9½ inch) china flan dish or tin.
3. Arrange the pecan nuts in circles on the bottom of the pastry case.
4. Whisk the eggs until light and frothy. Beat in the remaining ingredients and very carefully pour over the pecan nuts. They should stay in place.
5. Bake in the preheated oven at the higher temperature for 10 minutes, then reduce the heat and bake for a further 30 minutes. Allow to cool completely before serving.

Variation: For an extra nutty pie you can chop some more pecans, about 25–50g (1–2oz), and add these to the egg and syrup mixture. Pour this into the pastry case and then decorate with whole pecans. If pecans prove difficult to obtain, use walnuts instead.

SERVES 8
Nutrition content per serving   Carbohydrate: 56g   Fat: 22g
Fibre: 1g   Kilocalories: 427

Linzer torte; Pecan pie

PUFF-TOPPED RHUBARB PIE

SHORTCRUST PASTRY:
100g (4oz) plain flour
pinch of salt
25g (1oz) butter or margarine
25g (1oz) lard
about 1 tablespoon iced water
ROUGH PUFF PASTRY:
100g (4oz) plain flour
pinch of salt
75g (3oz) margarine, chilled
about 4 tablespoons iced water
milk or beaten egg, to glaze
sugar for dredging (optional)
FILLING:
750g (1½lb) rhubarb, trimmed and cut into chunks
about 100g (4oz) sugar
grated rind of ½ orange

Preparation time: about 1 hour, plus chilling
Cooking time: about 50 minutes
Oven: 220°C, 425°F, Gas Mark 7; then
190°C, 375°F, Gas Mark 5

1. To make the shortcrust pastry, sift the flour and salt into a bowl and rub in the butter and lard until the mixture resembles breadcrumbs. Add sufficient water to mix to a pliable dough. Wrap in polythene and chill.
2. Meanwhile, make the rough puff pastry. Sift the flour and salt into a bowl. Coarsely grate the chilled margarine into the flour and mix well. Add sufficient water to mix to a firm dough. On a floured surface, roll out the dough to a narrow strip; fold the bottom third up and the top third down. Seal the edges by pressing with a rolling pin, then give the dough a quarter turn so the folds are at the side.
3. Repeat the rolling out and folding twice more, then wrap the dough in polythene and chill for at least 20 minutes.
4. To make the filling, mix the rhubarb with the sugar and orange rind.
5. Roll out the shortcrust pastry and use to line a 22cm (8½ inch) pie dish or tin that is about 4cm (1½ inches) deep. Pack in the rhubarb tightly.
6. Roll out the rough puff pastry for the lid. Dampen the edges and place the lid in position. Press the edges well together to seal, and trim off any surplus dough. Flake the edge and scallop with the back of a knife, then decorate the top of the pie with the dough trimmings. Make a hole in the centre and brush all over with milk or beaten egg.
7. Bake in a preheated oven for 25–30 minutes or until lightly browned, then reduce the oven temperature and continue baking for 15–20 minutes or until the pastry is a rich golden brown.
8. Serve hot, sprinkled with sugar, with cream, custard or vanilla ice cream to accompany.

SERVES 6
Nutrition content per serving   Carbohydrate: 45g   Fat: 18g
Fibre: 4g   Kilocalories: 347

CROSTATA

3 recipe quantities rich sweet shortcrust pastry
(see Peach Cream Flan, page 53)
750g (1½lb) ricotta or sieved cottage cheese
100g (4oz) caster sugar
1 tablespoon plain flour
1 teaspoon salt
few drops of vanilla essence
finely grated rind of 1 orange
1 egg, separated
2 egg yolks
75g (3oz) sultanas
75g (3oz) chopped mixed peel
50g (2oz) pine nuts or slivered almonds

Preparation time: 45 minutes (including making pastry)
Cooking time: 1 hour
Oven: 180°C, 350°F, Gas Mark 4

1. Roll out two-thirds of the dough and use to line a greased 20–23cm (8–9 inch) loose-bottomed flan tin.
2. Mix the cheese with the caster sugar, flour, salt, vanilla essence, grated orange rind, 3 egg yolks, sultanas and mixed peel. Spread the cheese mixture evenly in the pastry case.
3. Roll out the remaining dough and cut into strips about 1cm (½ inch) wide. Criss-cross the strips over the cheese filling to give a lattice effect and pinch the ends of the strips to the edge of the pastry case. Whisk the egg white lightly and brush over the dough lattice. Sprinkle with the pine nuts or almonds.
4. Bake in a preheated oven for 1 hour or until the pastry is golden and the cheese filling firm. Allow to cool before unmoulding the crostata.

SERVES 8
Nutrition content per serving   Carbohydrate: 68g   Fat: 37g
Fibre: 3g   Kilocalories: 661

Puff-topped rhubarb pie; Crostata

COFFEE CHIFFON PIE

Crisp rich shortcrust pastry and a light fluffy mousse make a pleasing combination for this pie.

1 recipe quantity rich sweet shortcrust pastry
(see Peach Cream Flan, page 53)
15g (½oz) powdered gelatine
75ml (3floz) water
300ml (½ pint) milk
4 teaspoons instant coffee powder
65g (2½oz) sugar
2 eggs, separated
150ml (¼ pint) double or whipping cream, lightly whipped
DECORATION:
75ml (3floz) double or whipping cream, stiffly whipped
few walnut halves
chopped walnuts

Preparation time: 45 minutes, plus cooling
Cooking time: 20–25 minutes
Oven: 190°C, 375°F, Gas Mark 5

1. Roll out the pastry and use to line a 22cm (8½ inch) deep pie plate. Trim and flute the edge. Place in a preheated oven and bake blind for 25 minutes. Allow to cool.
2. Put the gelatine in a small heatproof bowl with the water and allow to soak for 5 minutes, then place in a pan of hot water to dissolve, stirring occasionally.
3. Heat the milk and coffee together until just below boiling. Add the sugar to the egg yolks and beat until thoroughly blended. Pour the hot milk on to the egg mixture and stir well, then return the custard to the pan and cook over a gentle heat until it thickens slightly. The custard will just coat the back of a metal spoon when thick enough.
4. Add the dissolved gelatine to the custard. Strain into a bowl and leave to cool.
5. When the custard is on the point of setting, whisk the egg whites until stiff and fold the cream and then the egg whites into the custard. Pour into the cold pastry case and allow to set.
6. To decorate, spoon the cream into a piping bag fitted with a large star nozzle and pipe the edge of the pie with rosettes of cream. Decorate with the walnut halves and chopped walnuts and serve cold. Eat on the same day.

SERVES 8
Nutrition content per serving   Carbohydrate: 23g   Fat: 23g
Fibre: trace   Kilocalories: 317

Coffee chiffon pie; Cumberland rum nicky

CUMBERLAND RUM NICKY

Cumberland rum butter is a delicious hard sauce made with butter, brown sugar and rum and is served with Christmas pudding and mince pies instead of brandy butter in many parts of the country. In this sweet pie a similar mixture is used to flavour the unusual date and ginger filling.

100g (4oz) stoned dates, chopped
50g (2oz) preserved ginger, chopped
1 cooking apple, peeled, cored and chopped
50g (2oz) butter, at room temperature
25g (1oz) soft brown sugar
2 teaspoons grated lemon rind
2 tablespoons rum
icing sugar, to finish
RICH SWEET SHORTCRUST PASTRY:
225g (8oz) plain flour
pinch of salt
50g (2oz) butter
50g (2oz) lard
25g (1oz) caster sugar
1 egg yolk

Preparation time: 35 minutes
Cooking time: 30–35 minutes
Oven: 220°C, 425°F, Gas Mark 7; then
190°C, 375°F, Gas Mark 5

1. For the pastry, sift the flour and salt into a mixing bowl. Cut in the fat, then rub in with the fingertips until the mixture resembles breadcrumbs. Add the sugar, then mix in the egg yolk and enough iced water to bind to a firm dough. Knead lightly until smooth and rest well before rolling it out.
2. Mix together the chopped dates, ginger and apple. Cream the butter with the sugar and lemon rind and gradually beat in the rum.
3. Divide the pastry in half and roll out one half thinly. Use to line a 20cm (8 inch) shallow round pie dish. Cover the bottom with the mixed dates, ginger and apple. Spread the creamed mixture over the filling. Roll out the remaining pastry to make a lid. Knock back the edge of the pastry and pinch into flutes. Cut V-shaped slits in the top of the pie to allow the steam to escape.
4. Bake in a preheated oven for 10–15 minutes. Reduce the heat and bake for a further 20 minutes or until the pastry is crisp and golden. Remove from the oven and dust with sifted icing sugar. This pie is usually served hot.

SERVES 6
Nutrition content per serving   Carbohydrate: 58g   Fat: 23g
Fibre: 3g   Kilocalories: 458

CANADIAN RAISIN PIE

175g (6oz) soft brown sugar
2 tablespoons plain flour
pinch of salt
350g (12oz) raisins
450ml (¾ pint) water
2 tablespoons maple or golden syrup
finely grated rind and juice of 1 lemon
PASTRY:
275g (10oz) plain flour
pinch of salt
2 teaspoons baking powder
75g (3oz) caster sugar
¼ teaspoon vanilla essence
1 egg, separated
1 tablespoon milk
150g (5oz) butter or margarine

Preparation time: 45 minutes, plus chilling
Cooking time: 30 minutes
Oven: 200°C, 400°F, Gas Mark 6

1. To make the filling: put all the ingredients in a pan. Bring to the boil, then lower the heat and simmer for about 10 minutes until the raisins are plump and the mixture is thick, stirring frequently. Remove from the heat and leave to cool.
2. Meanwhile, make the pastry: sift the flour, salt and baking powder into a bowl. Make a well in the centre and put in the sugar, vanilla essence, half the egg yolk, all the egg white and the milk. Stir the ingredients together until evenly mixed, then add the butter or margarine in pieces and beat quickly into the flour mixture. Knead lightly to form a smooth dough, wrap and chill in the refrigerator for 30 minutes.
3. Roll out half of the dough on a lightly floured surface, and use to line a 23cm (9 inch) flan dish. Spoon the filling into the dish. Roll out the remaining dough to make a lid. Prick the lid with a fork, then brush with the remaining egg yolk mixed with a little milk.
4. Bake in a preheated oven for 30 minutes or until the pastry is golden brown. Remove from the oven and leave to cool for 15 minutes. Serve warm or cold.

SERVES 8
Nutrition content per serving   Carbohydrate: 82g   Fat: 17g
Fibre: 4g   Kilocalories: 477

APPLE FLORENTINE PIE

An eighteenth-century recipe from Lincolnshire and Bedfordshire, this is traditionally made at Christmas.

4 large cooking apples
3 tablespoons demerara sugar
1 tablespoon grated lemon rind
50g (2oz) sultanas
600ml (1 pint) pale ale
¼ teaspoon grated nutmeg
¼ teaspoon ground cinnamon
3 cloves
whipped cream, to serve
SHORTCRUST PASTRY:
225g (8oz) plain flour
¼ teaspoon salt
100g (4oz) butter or margarine
50ml (2floz) iced water

Preparation time: 30 minutes
Cooking time: 30 minutes
Oven: 200°C, 400°F, Gas Mark 6

1. To make the pastry, sift the flour and salt into a bowl, cut in the butter or margarine and rub in with the fingertips until the mixture resembles breadcrumbs. Mix in enough water to bind to a soft, not sticky, dough. Roll out to 1cm (½ inch) thick on a floured board.
2. Peel and core the apples, stand in a deep, buttered pie dish and sprinkle with 2 tablespoons of the sugar and 1 teaspoon of grated lemon rind. Fill the centre of each apple with sultanas.
3. Cover with the pastry and bake in a preheated oven for 30 minutes.
4. Heat together, but do not boil, the ale, nutmeg, cinnamon, cloves and remaining sugar and lemon rind.
5. Carefully loosen the crust and lift the pastry off the apples. Pour the ale mixture over the apples. Cut the pastry into 4 pieces and place one on each apple.
6. Serve very hot in bowls. Whipped cream is delicious with this.

SERVES 4
Nutrition content per serving   Carbohydrate: 79g   Fat: 21g
Fibre: 7g   Kilocalories: 550

Canadian raisin pie; Apple florentine pie

LITTLE CAKES
& PASTRIES

*Individual portions of cake or pastry are very
appealing, and are ideal for offering at teatime, for
picnics and packed lunches, and for quick snacks. They
make easy-to-serve desserts too. Many little cakes and
pastries are also very pretty, and can be imaginatively
decorated. The recipes in this chapter range from pastries
to be served as soon as they are fried or baked, to little
cakes that can be kept in an airtight tin, ready to be
enjoyed at any time.*

PEARS EN CHEMISE

6 large firm cooking pears (Conference type)
4 tablespoons raisins
3 tablespoons soft brown sugar
¼ teaspoon ground cinnamon
2 teaspoons rum essence (optional)
400g (14oz) puff pastry, thawed if frozen
½ egg, lightly beaten
2 tablespoons caster sugar

Preparation time: 35 minutes
Cooking time: 40–50 minutes
Oven: 190°C, 375°F, Gas Mark 5

1. Peel the pears, then core them carefully from the bottom end and trim the bottoms so that the pears will stand upright. Do not remove the stalks.
2. Mix together the raisins, brown sugar, cinnamon and rum essence (if using), then fill the cavities in the pears with this mixture.
3. Roll out the pastry on a lightly floured surface, trim the edges and cut into 6 squares. Stand a pear on each square, then fold the pastry around the pear to enclose it completely. Use the trimmings of pastry to make a 'cap' for each pear. Leave the stalk protruding at the top of each pear.
4. Stand the pears upright on a damp baking sheet. Brush all over with the beaten egg and sprinkle with the caster sugar. Bake in a preheated oven for 40–50 minutes or until the pastry is golden brown and the pears feel soft when pierced with a skewer.
5. Serve warm with cream or thin pouring custard.

SERVES 6
Nutrition content per serving   Carbohydrate: 54g   Fat: 16g
Fibre: 7g   Kilocalories: 370

CREAM SLICES

225g (8oz) puff pastry, thawed if frozen
GLACÉ ICING:
100g (4oz) icing sugar
1–2 tablespoons warm water or lemon juice
FILLING:
6 tablespoons raspberry jam
150ml (¼ pint) double cream, lightly whipped

Preparation time: 25 minutes, plus resting
Cooking time: 15–20 minutes
Oven: 230°C, 450°F, Gas Mark 8

1. Roll out the pastry on a floured surface to a rectangle and trim to 30 × 25cm (12 × 10 inches). Cut in half lengthways. For one large cream slice, transfer the two rectangles to dampened or lightly greased baking sheets. For individual slices, cut each rectangle of dough into 13 × 5cm (5 × 2 inch) strips and place on baking sheets. Leave to rest for 10 minutes.
2. Bake in a preheated oven for 15–20 minutes or until well risen and golden brown. Cool on wire trays. Select the best large piece, or 6 small pieces, of pastry to be iced for the tops.
3. To make the glacé icing, sift the icing sugar into a bowl and beat in sufficient warm water or lemon juice to give a thick coating consistency. Spread the white icing evenly over the best pieces of pastry. Leave to set.
4. To assemble the cream slices, spread the pastry base or bases with jam and then with whipped cream. Position the iced tops, pressing down gently to give an even shape. The large cream slice can then be cut carefully into six slices.

SERVES 6
Nutrition content per serving   Carbohydrate: 42g   Fat: 21g
Fibre: 1g   Kilocalories: 357

SUFFOLK CAKES

100g (4oz) butter
4 eggs, separated
225g (8oz) caster sugar
grated rind of ½ lemon
100g (4oz) self-raising flour

Preparation time: 10 minutes
Cooking time: 15 minutes
Oven: 200°C, 400°F, Gas Mark 6

1. Grease 14 bun tins or patty pans.
2. Warm the butter so that it is just liquid but not at all coloured.
3. Beat the egg whites until they just hold a peak.
4. Beat the egg yolks, add the sugar and grated lemon rind and fold into the beaten whites.
5. Beat in the butter and stir in the flour. Beat well and turn into the prepared tins.
6. Bake in a preheated oven for 10–15 minutes.

MAKES ABOUT 14
Nutrition content per serving   Carbohydrate: 22g   Fat: 8g
Fibre: 0g   Kilocalories: 165

Clockwise from the top: Pears en chemise; Suffolk cakes; Cream slices

APRICOT & RAISIN ENVELOPES

75g (3oz) dried apricots, chopped
75g (3oz) raisins
300ml (½ pint) water
75g (3oz) ground almonds
ROUGH PUFF PASTRY:
200g (8oz) plain flour
½ teaspoon salt
75g (3oz) lard
75g (3oz) butter or margarine
2 teaspoons lemon juice
120ml (4floz) iced water
milk, to glaze

Preparation time: 1½ hours, plus chilling
Cooking time: 25 minutes
Oven: 220°C, 425°F, Gas Mark 7

1. To make the pastry, sift the flour and salt into a bowl. Cut the fats into small pieces and toss in the flour to coat them.
2. Add the lemon juice and water and mix lightly with a round-ended knife to make a soft lumpy dough. Place the dough on a floured surface and shape into a square.
3. Roll out the dough, using short forward strokes, to an oblong 36 × 13cm (15 × 5 inches). Fold up the bottom third of the dough and the top third down to cover it. Press the edges together to seal. Give the dough a quarter turn and roll and fold as before. Sprinkle the dough with flour and place in a polythene bag. Chill for 20 minutes.
4. Repeat the rolling and folding twice more, and chill for a further 30 minutes before using.
5. Meanwhile, place the apricots, raisins and water in a saucepan. Bring to the boil, reduce the heat, cover and cook gently for 20 minutes, until soft and pulpy. Remove from the heat and stir in the ground almonds. Leave to cool.
6. Roll out the pastry and trim to a 40 × 30cm (16 × 12 inch) oblong. Cut into twelve 10cm (4 inch) squares.
7. Pile the filling into the centre of each square. Dampen the edges of the pastry. Draw up the corners to the centre and press the edges to seal. Flute the edges.
8. Place the envelopes on a baking sheet and brush with milk. Bake in a preheated oven for 25 minutes, until golden brown.

MAKES 12
Nutrition content per serving   Carbohydrate: 21g   Fat: 15g
Fibre: 3g   Kilocalories: 226

ALMOND BUNS

These little buns have a rich centre of almond paste, and are topped with flaked almonds.

175g (6oz) plain flour
½ teaspoon baking powder
pinch of salt
75g (3oz) butter or margarine
50g (2oz) caster sugar
1 egg, beaten
ALMOND PASTE:
50g (2oz) ground almonds
25g (1oz) caster sugar
25g (1oz) icing sugar
1 egg yolk
squeeze of lemon juice
TOPPING:
1 egg white, beaten
flaked almonds

Preparation time: 40 minutes
Cooking time: 15 minutes
Oven: 220°C, 425°F, Gas Mark 7

1. Sift the flour, baking powder and salt into a mixing bowl. Cut the fat into the flour and rub in with the fingertips until the mixture resembles breadcrumbs. Stir in the sugar and bind into a stiff dough with the beaten egg, adding a spoonful of iced water if necessary.
2. To make the almond paste, mix together the ground almonds and sugars. Bind with the egg yolk into a stiff paste, and flavour to taste with the lemon juice. Roll into 16 marbles using sugared fingers.
3. Roll the dough into a sausage shape and divide into 16 equal portions. Shape into balls on a floured board and flatten slightly.
4. Place a marble of almond paste in the centre of each bun and gather the edges together over it. Turn upside down and place on a greased baking sheet. Brush the buns with the beaten egg white and sprinkle with flaked almonds.
5. Bake in a preheated oven for 15 minutes or until well risen and golden brown. Cool on a wire tray.

MAKES 16
Nutrition content per serving   Carbohydrate: 15g   Fat: 7g
Fibre: 1g   Kilocalories: 126

Apricot & raisin envelopes; Almond buns

BUTTERSCOTCH NUT BROWNIES

50g (2oz) butter or margarine
225g (8oz) soft brown sugar
1 egg, beaten
¼ teaspoon vanilla essence
50g (2oz) plain flour
1 teaspoon baking powder
½ teaspoon salt
100g (4oz) mixed shelled hazelnuts and walnuts,
coarsely chopped

Preparation time: 15 minutes
Cooking time: 30 minutes
Oven: 190°C, 375°F, Gas Mark 5

1. Grease and line the bottom of a shallow 20cm (8 inch) square tin.
2. Melt the fat in a saucepan over gentle heat, then mix in the sugar. Cool slightly, and beat in the egg and vanilla essence. Sift the flour together with the baking powder and salt and mix in thoroughly. Stir in the nuts.
3. Pour into the prepared tin. Bake in a preheated oven for about 30 minutes or until set, but not hard.
4. Cut into 16 squares while still hot, then allow to cool in the tin. When cold, lift out carefully and store in an airtight or plastic container.

MAKES 16
Nutrition content per serving   Carbohydrate: 16g   Fat: 6g
Fibre: 0.5g   Kilocalories: 119

CHERRY BUMPERS

When cherries are out of season use a can of pie filling and omit step 1.

350g (12oz) ripe sweet cherries, stoned
50g (2oz) sugar
1 tablespoon water
1 recipe quantity shortcrust pastry (see Apple
Florentine Pie, page 64)
milk to glaze

*Preparation time: 35 minutes, plus cooling (including
making pastry)*
Cooking time: 20–25 minutes
Oven: 200°C, 400°F, Gas Mark 6

1. Place the cherries, sugar and water in a saucepan. Cook gently, stirring occasionally, until the cherries are softened, about 5 minutes. Leave to cool.
2. Roll out the pastry and cut into twelve 10cm (4 inch) rounds. Divide the cherries between the rounds and dampen the edges of the pastry.
3. Draw up the pastry over the filling and press the edges to seal, making tricorn or Cornish pasty shapes. Flute the joins by pinching with the fingers.
4. Place the bumpers on a baking sheet and brush with milk. Bake in a preheated oven for 20–25 minutes until golden brown. Serve warm or cold.

MAKES 12
Nutrition content per serving   Carbohydrate: 19g   Fat: 7g
Fibre: 1g   Kilocalories: 144

CHESTNUT BOATS

½ recipe quantity rich sweet shortcrust pastry
(see Pecan Pie, page 59)
225g (8oz) unsweetened chestnut purée
25-50g (1–2oz) caster sugar
3 tablespoons brandy
6 tablespoons double or whipping cream, stiffly
whipped
DECORATION:
glacé cherries
crystallized angelica

Preparation time: 45 minutes (including making pastry)
Cooking time: 10–12 minutes
Oven: 190°C, 375°F, Gas Mark 5

1. Roll out the pastry thinly and use to line 9.5cm (3¾ inch) boat-shaped tartlet tins or barquette moulds. Prick the pastry well, place in a preheated oven and bake blind for 10–12 minutes. Remove carefully from the tins and cool on a wire tray.
2. Blend the chestnut purée, caster sugar and brandy together in a bowl until the sugar has dissolved. Fold the cream into the mixture.
3. Spoon the chestnut cream into a piping bag fitted with a large star nozzle and pipe a wavy line down the centre of each pastry boat. Decorate the centre of each boat with a small piece of glacé cherry and 2 angelica leaves. When filled, eat on the same day.

MAKES 20
Nutrition content per serving   Carbohydrate: 21g   Fat: 9g
Fibre: 2g   Kilocalories: 171

*Clockwise from the top: Butterscotch nut brownies; Chestnut boats;
Cherry bumpers*

ENGLISH MADELEINES

These little cakes look so pretty on the tea table, yet they're simple to make with a victoria sandwich mix.

100g (4oz) butter, at room temperature
100g (4oz) caster sugar
2 eggs, beaten
100g (4oz) self-raising flour
pinch of salt
about 1 tablespoon warm water
TO FINISH:
4–6 tablespoons red fruit jam, sieved
4 tablespoons desiccated coconut
about 6 glacé cherries, halved
few snips candied angelica

Preparation time: 25 minutes, plus cooling
Cooking time: 15–20 minutes
Oven: 180°C, 350°F, Gas Mark 4

1. Grease and flour 12 dariole or castle pudding moulds.
2. Cream together the butter and sugar until light fluffy. Beat in the eggs.
3. Sift the flour and salt. Stir 1 tablespoon of flour into the butter mixture until well mixed. Gradually fold in the remaining flour. Add enough water to give the mixture a soft dropping consistency.
4. Divide the mixture equally between the prepared moulds.
5. Bake just above centre in a preheated oven for 15–20 minutes or until well risen and golden.
6. Turn the madeleines carefully out of the moulds, upside down, and leave to cool. Trim the bases if they do not stand up well.
7. When cool, brush with the sieved jam, then roll in the coconut. Stand upright on a serving plate and decorate the top of each with a halved glacé cherry and two angelica 'leaves'.

MAKES 12
Nutrition contennt per serving   Carbohydrate: 24g   Fat: 11g
Fibre: 1g   Kilocalories: 198

Below: English madeleines
Opposite top: Truffle cakes
Opposite bottom: Churros

CHURROS

175g (6oz) plain flour
pinch of salt
300ml (½ pint) water
100g (4oz) butter
3 eggs, beaten
groundnut or sunflower oil for deep frying
caster sugar mixed with ground cinnamon, for dredging

Preparation time: 15 minutes
Cooking time: 3–4 minutes

1. Sift the flour and salt on to a sheet of greaseproof paper. Put the water and butter in a pan and heat gently until the butter has melted. Bring to the boil and, when bubbling vigorously, remove from the heat and immediately add the flour all at once. Beat well with a wooden spoon until the mixture forms a ball and draws away from the sides of the pan.
2. Leave the mixture to cool until lukewarm, then beat in the eggs gradually until the mixture is smooth and glossy.
3. Put the mixture into a large piping bag fitted with a large rose nozzle.
4. Heat the oil in a large saucepan to 180°C (350°F) or test by dropping in a 1cm (½ inch) cube of bread. It should turn golden in 30 seconds.
5. Pipe sections of dough approximately 10cm (4 inches) long into the hot oil and fry them until golden brown.
6. Remove the churros from the pan with a slotted spoon, drain on paper towels and toss in cinnamon sugar. Serve immediately.

SERVES 6
Nutrition content per serving   Carbohydrate: 25g   Fat: 22g
Fibre: 1g   Kilocalories: 322

TRUFFLE CAKES

225g (8oz) plain chocolate, broken into pieces
50g (2oz) dry cake crumbs
50g (2oz) Nice, digestive or ginger biscuits, crushed
25g (1oz) glacé cherries, chopped
2 tablespoons apricot jam
1 tablespoon coffee essence or strong black coffee
DECORATION:
150ml (¼ pint) double or whipping cream
4 glacé cherries, halved
8 chocolate leaves

Preparation time: 25 minutes, plus chilling
Cooking time: about 5 minutes

1. Melt the chocolate in a heatproof bowl over hot water.
2. Using a pastry brush, coat the insides of eight paper cake cases with half the melted chocolate. Chill until set, then add a second layer of chocolate. Chill for several hours or overnight until very firm.
3. Mix together the cake and biscuit crumbs. Add the cherries and bind together with the jam and coffee essence or coffee.
4. Carefully peel the paper from the chocolate cases and arrange them on a plate. Fill with the cake mixture.
5. Whip the cream until stiff. Pipe a whirl of cream on top of the filling in each chocolate cup. Complete with half a glacé cherry and a chocolate leaf.

MAKES 8
Nutrition content per serving   Carbohydrate: 33g   Fat: 19g
Fibre: 1g   Kilocalories: 304

GLACÉ CHERRY TARTLETS

SHORTCRUST PASTRY:
100g (4oz) plain flour
pinch of salt
50g (2oz) plain wholewheat flour
40g (1½oz) butter or margarine
40g (1½oz) lard
FILLING:
100g (4oz) redcurrant, seedless raspberry or
cranberry jelly
100g (4oz) glacé cherries
50g (2oz) butter or margarine, at room temperature
50g (2oz) light soft brown sugar
1 egg (size 1 or 2)
50g (2oz) self-raising flour
1 teaspoon water
a few drops of almond essence
DECORATION:
100g (4oz) icing sugar, sifted
1–2 tablespoons strained lemon juice
6 glacé cherries, washed and dried
about 25g (1oz) blanched almonds, chopped and
toasted

Preparation time: about 45 mintues
Cooking time: about 25 minutes
Oven: 200°C, 400°F, Gas Mark 6

1. Put a baking sheet into a preheated oven to heat while preparing the tartlets.
2. For the pastry: sift the plain flour and salt into a bowl, then mix in the wholewheat flour. Add the fats and rub in until the mixture resembles fine breadcrumbs. Add sufficient iced water to mix to a pliable dough.
3. Knead the dough lightly until smooth, then roll out and use to line 6 individual flan tins or rings or individual Yorkshire pudding tins 10–11cm (4–4½ inches) in diameter.
4. Spread a thin layer of jelly in the base of each pastry case. Reserve the 6 best cherries and slice the remainder; divide between the pastry cases.
5. Cream the butter or margarine and sugar together until light and fluffy. Beat in the egg. Sift the flour into the mixture and fold in. Add the water and almond essence.
6. Divide the mixture between the pastry cases and spread out evenly but lightly to cover the cherries.
7. Stand the tins on the hot baking sheet, return to the oven and bake for 25 minutes or until golden brown and firm.
8. Remove carefully from the tins and cool on a wire tray.
9. Before serving, blend the icing sugar with sufficient lemon juice to give a smooth thick spreading consistency and spread over the tartlets. Add a cherry and sprinkle with toasted nuts. Leave to set.

MAKES 6
Nutrition content per serving   Carbohydrate: 74g   Fat: 23g
Fibre: 2g   Kilocalories: 507

APPLE & DATE SLICES

350g (12oz) cooking apples, peeled, cored and roughly chopped
100g (4oz) stoned dates, chopped
50g (2oz) shelled walnuts, chopped
50g (2oz) brown sugar
WHOLEMEAL SHORTCRUST PASTRY:
225g (8oz) wholemeal flour
pinch of salt
50g (2oz) butter or margarine
50g (2oz) lard
about 4 tablespoons iced water
TOPPING:
225g (8oz) wholemeal flour
100g (4oz) butter or margarine
25g (1oz) soft brown sugar
¼ teaspoon ground cinnamon

Preparation time: 35 minutes
Cooking time: 40 minutes
Oven: 200°C, 400°F, Gas Mark 6

1. To make the pastry, put the flour and salt into a bowl. Cut in the fats, then rub in until the mixture resembles breadcrumbs. Mix in enough water to bind to a soft, not sticky dough.
2. Roll out the dough and use to line a greased 18 × 28cm (7 × 11 inch) shallow tin. Trim the edges.
3. Place the apples, dates, walnuts and brown sugar in a bowl and stir together. Spread in an even layer in the pastry case.
4. For the topping, put the flour into a bowl and rub in the butter or margarine. When finely mixed, blend in the sugar and cinnamon. Sprinkle in a layer to cover the topping.
5. Place in a preheated oven and bake for 40 minutes. Remove from the oven and cut into 16 slices. Allow to cool slightly, then remove from the tin and place on a wire tray until cold.

MAKES 16
Nutrition content per serving   Carbohydrate: 29g   Fat: 13g
Fibre: 4g   Kilocalories: 241

Glacé cherry tartlets (top); Apple & date slices

NUTTY MERINGUES

2 egg whites (size 1 or 2)
150g (5oz) icing sugar, sifted
50g (2oz) shelled hazelnuts or almonds, toasted and
finely chopped

Preparation time: about 15 minutes
Cooking time: about 30 minutes
Oven: 150°C, 300°F, Gas Mark 2

1. Put the egg whites and sugar into a heatproof bowl over a saucepan of gently simmering water and whisk until the mixture thickens and stands in stiff peaks.
2. Remove from the heat and beat in the hazelnuts or almonds.
3. Spoon the mixture into rounds about 5–6cm (2–2½ inches) in diameter on baking sheets lined with non-stick silicone paper or rice paper.
4. Bake in a preheated oven for about 30 minutes or until pale cream in colour and easily removed from the sheets. Leave to cool, then store in an airtight container.
5. Serve plain or topped with a whirl of whipped cream and a piece of soft fruit or a hazelnut. Alternatively, drizzle with melted chocolate.

MAKES 10
Nutrition content per serving   Carbohydrate: 16g   Fat: 2g
Fibre: 0g   Kilocalories: 81

CREAM HORNS

225g (8oz) plain flour
pinch of salt
75g (3oz) butter or margarine
150ml (¼ pint) iced water
75g (3oz) lard
lightly whisked egg white, or water
1 tablespoon caster sugar
2 tablespoons raspberry jam
250ml (8floz) double or whipping cream, whipped

Preparation time: 1½ hours, plus chilling
Cooking time: 15–20 minutes
Oven: 220°C, 425°F, Gas Mark 7

1. Sift the flour and salt into a bowl. Cut in half the butter or margarine and rub the fat into the flour with the fingertips until the mixture resembles fine crumbs. Add the water and work in lightly using a knife. A little more water can be added if necessary to bind the dough together to a soft but not sticky consistency.
2. Shape the dough into a rectangle on a lightly floured surface, then roll out into an oblong about 41cm (16 inches) long. Ease any rounded corners into shape. Mark lightly into thirds.
3. Using a round ended knife, dab half the lard in rough heaps on the top two-thirds of the pastry, leaving a border around the edge. Fold the lower third up over the centre section, then fold the top third down over this, keeping the corners square. Seal the edges with the rolling pin and give the pastry a half turn so that the fold is at the right hand side.
4. Roll out the pastry as before and repeat the process, first using the rest of the butter and then using the remaining lard. Roll and fold once more without the addition of any more fat.
5. Wrap and chill in the refrigerator for 20 minutes or longer before use. As the pastry needs to be cool all the time it is being made, it can be chilled between rollings during hot weather.
6. Roll out the pastry thinly to a 45 × 30cm (18 × 12 inch) rectangle. Trim the edges and cut lengthways into 10 strips. Cut a small piece diagonally from one end of each strip to make a point. Brush the strips with water.
7. Place the point of a cream horn tin against the point of a pastry strip. Wind the strip around the tin so that it overlaps about 1cm (½ inch) at each turn. Place on a dampened baking sheet. When all the horns have been shaped, put in the refrigerator for 20 minutes to rest.
8. Brush with lightly whisked egg white or water and sprinkle with the sugar. Place in a preheated oven and bake for 15–20 minutes until golden brown. Remove the horns from the tins with a slight twisting action. Cool on a wire tray.
9. Heat the jam until it has melted and, with a teaspoon, pour a little into the point of each horn. When the pastry and the jam are completely cold, spoon the cream into a piping bag fitted with a large rosette nozzle and fill each horn with a large swirl of cream. Keep cool until served. When filled, eat on the same day.

MAKES 10
Nutrition content per serving   Carbohydrate: 21g   Fat: 26g
Fibre: 1g   Kilocalories: 324

Nutty meringues; Cream horns

LEMON CURD & CARAWAY CAKES

These delightful cakes are quick and easy to make, either by hand or with the mixer. They are delicious plain, but can be topped with lemon glacé icing.

150g (5oz) soft tub margarine
100g (4oz) caster sugar
150g (5oz) lemon curd
225g (8oz) self-raising flour
pinch of salt
1 teaspoon caraway seeds
3 eggs, beaten

Preparation time: 15 minutes
Cooking time: 20 minutes
Oven: 180°C, 350°F, Gas Mark 4

1. Grease bun tins or patty pans.
2. Cream the margarine and sugar together until light and fluffy. Beat in the lemon curd. Sift the flour and salt and mix in the caraway seeds. Beat the eggs into the creamed mixture, one at a time, with 2 tablespoons flour each time. Fold in the remaining flour.
3. Spoon the mixture into the prepared tins until three-quarters full. Bake in a preheated oven for 20 minutes, until golden and firm to the touch.
4. Allow the cakes to cool and shrink slightly, then remove from tins and cool completely on a wire tray.

MAKES ABOUT 30
Nutrition content per serving   Carbohydrate: 11g   Fat: 6g
Fibre: 0g   Kilocalories: 98

PROFITEROLES WITH BANANA CREAM

65g (2½oz) plain flour
pinch of salt
150ml (¼ pint) water
50g (2oz) butter or margarine
2 eggs, beaten
CHOCOLATE SAUCE:
100g (4oz) plain chocolate, broken into pieces
2 tablespoons brandy or water
50g (2oz) icing sugar, sifted
25g (1oz) unsalted butter
FILLING:
300ml (½ pint) double cream
1 banana
25g (1oz) icing sugar, sifted

Preparation time: 30 minutes, plus cooling
Cooking time: 15–20 minutes
Oven: 220°C, 425°F, Gas Mark 7

1. Sift the flour and salt on to a sheet of greaseproof paper. Put the water in a pan with the butter or margarine and heat gently until the fat has melted. Bring to the boil and, when bubbling vigorously, remove from the heat and immediately add the flour all at once. Beat well with a wooden spoon until the mixture forms a ball and draws away from the sides of the pan.
2. Leave the mixture to cool until lukewarm, then beat in the eggs a little at a time until the pastry is smooth and glossy and has a piping consistency.
3. Put the choux paste in a piping bag fitted with a 1cm (½ inch) plain nozzle and pipe about 24 small rounds on lightly greased baking sheets. Space the rounds well apart to allow for expansion during cooking.
4. Bake just above the centre of a preheated oven for 15–20 minutes.
5. Meanwhile, make the chocolate sauce: put all the ingredients in a heatproof bowl placed over a pan of gently simmering water. Heat gently until the ingredients are melted and a smooth sauce is formed, stirring with a wooden spoon. Remove from the heat, pour into a serving jug and leave to cool.
6. When the profiteroles are well risen and golden brown, remove from the baking sheets. Make a slit in the side of each profiterole, then leave them to cool on a wire tray.
7. To make the filling, whip the cream until it holds its shape. Peel the banana, mash with the icing sugar, then fold into the whipped cream.
8. To serve, put the banana cream in a piping bag fitted with a small nozzle, then pipe into the

profiteroles through the slits in the sides. Pile the profiteroles up on a serving plate, then pour over the chocolate sauce and serve immediately.

Above: Profiteroles with banana cream
Opposite: Lemon curd & caraway cakes

SERVES 6

Nutrition content per serving   Carbohydrate: 37g   Fat: 41g
Fibre: 1g   Kilocalories: 544

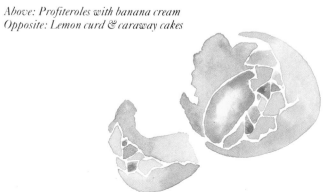

CRANBERRY-APPLE STRUDELS

The strudels can be made smaller if preferred by cutting each half of the dough into 6 instead of 4 strips. Complete in the same way.

225g (8oz) plain flour
½ teaspoon salt
1 egg, beaten
2 tablespoons oil
85ml (3floz) lukewarm water
icing sugar, to dredge
a little extra ground cinnamon
FILLING:
900g (2lb) cooking apples
225g (8oz) cranberries, fresh or
frozen and thawed
½ teaspoon ground cinnamon
about 4 tablespoons water
sugar to taste
50g (2oz) butter, melted
100g (4oz) ground almonds

Preparation time: about 1 hour, plus resting
Cooking time: 35–40 minutes
Oven: 190°C, 375°F, Gas Mark 5

1. Sift the flour and salt into a bowl and make a well in the centre.
2. Add the egg, oil and water and mix together gradually to make a soft, sticky dough. If it feels too sticky, add a sprinkling of flour. Work the dough until it leaves the sides of the bowl clean.
3. Turn on to a lightly floured surface and knead for about 15 minutes or until the dough no longer sticks to the hands or board. Shape into a ball and put on to a cloth; cover with the bowl and leave in a warm place to rest for 1 hour.
4. For the filling: peel, core and slice the apples and put into a saucepan with the cranberries, cinnamon and water. Cover and simmer gently for about 10 minutes or until soft. Beat in sugar to taste and leave to get cold.
5. Warm a wooden rolling pin and spread a clean cloth on a large flat working surface or table. Dredge lightly with flour.
6. Put the dough on to the cloth and roll out carefully into a square about 3mm (⅛ inch) thick. Lift the dough and turn it frequently so that it does not stick to the cloth.
7. Using the backs of the hands, under the dough, gently lift and stretch it, beginning in the centre and working out to the edge, until it is paper thin and measures about 80cm (32 inches) square. Neaten the edges with a sharp knife and leave to rest for 15 minutes.
8. Brush the dough all over with most of the melted butter, then sprinkle with ground almonds. Cut the dough in half and then each piece into 4 equal oblongs by cutting at right angles to the first cut.
9. Divide the fruit mixture between the pieces of dough, spreading it to within 2.5cm (1 inch) of two long sides and one short side and 7.5cm (3 inches) of the other short side. Fold the narrow edges over the filling and, beginning at the narrow end, roll up towards the wide border, keeping it neat and even. Place the parcels on greased baking sheets, keeping the join underneath.
10. Brush with melted butter and bake in a preheated oven for 25–30 minutes or until golden brown. Remove to a wire tray. When cool, dredge with icing sugar flavoured with a little ground cinnamon.

SERVES 8
Nutrition content per serving   Carbohydrate: 34g   Fat: 17g
Fibre: 6g   Kilocalories: 302

PLUM & ORANGE PIES

1½ recipe quantities shortcrust pastry (see Gooseberry
& Orange Plate Pie, page 57)
225g (8oz) plums, stoned and quartered
25g (1oz) caster sugar
finely grated rind of ½ orange
large pinch of ground cinnamon
2 teaspoons cornflour
milk, to glaze

Preparation time: 30 minutes (including making pastry)
Cooking time: 20–25 minutes
Oven: 200°C, 400°F, Gas Mark 6

1. Divide the dough in half and roll out one half. Use to line 8 barquette (boat-shaped) tins.
2. Mix together the plums, sugar, orange rind, cinnamon and cornflour. Divide the fruit filling between the lined tins.
3. Roll out the remaining dough and cut out ovals for lids. Moisten the edges of the dough with water. Place the lids over the fruit and press on to seal well. Brush with milk.
4. Bake in a preheated oven for 20-25 minutes. Serve warm or cold.

MAKES 8
Nutrition content per serving   Carbohydrate: 24g   Fat: 9g
Fibre: 1g   Kilocalories: 186

Cranberry-apple strudels (top); Plum & orange pies

BISCUITS & COOKIES

A never-empty tin of deliciously-fresh homemade biscuits and cookies must be everyone's wish – and it's a wish that can be granted because most biscuits and cookies are quick to make. Whether crisp and crunchy, chewy, or meltingly tender, biscuits and cookies are always welcome, and they make even a simple cup of tea into a special treat. The recipes in this chapter include both easy biscuits and cookies and more difficult, time-consuming ones for special occasions.

HONEY & ORANGE BRANDYSNAPS

100g (4oz) unsalted butter
100g (4oz) caster sugar
100g (4oz) clear honey
grated rind of 1 orange
1 tablespoon brandy
100g (4oz) plain flour

Preparation time: 30 minutes
Cooking time: 10 minutes
Oven: 190°C, 375°F, Gas Mark 5

1. Line three baking sheets with non-stick silicone paper.
2. Heat the butter, sugar, honey and orange rind in a pan over a low heat. When melted, add the brandy. Away from the heat, stir in the flour and work to a smooth paste.
3. Place a heaped teaspoon of the mixture on the prepared baking sheet. Flatten into an oblong shape with a knife dipped in hot water. Repeat the procedure with the remaining mixture so there are 6-7 biscuits on each baking sheet, leaving a good space between each one to allow for spreading. Bake in a preheated oven for 10 minutes or until golden.
4. Remove from the oven and cool for 30 seconds, then lift a brandysnap off the silicone paper with a palette knife. Curl it around a thick-handled wooden spoon, let set and then slide off on to a wire tray to cool. If the brandysnaps harden before you shape them all, return them to the oven for a few seconds to soften.

MAKES ABOUT 20
Nutrition content per serving   Carbohydrate: 13g   Fat: 4g
Fibre: trace   Kilocalories: 90

PIPED BISCUITS

100g (4oz) soft tub margarine
25g (1oz) icing sugar, sifted
75g (3oz) plain flour
25g (1oz) cornflour
few drops of vanilla essence
glacé cherries and angelica, to decorate

Preparation time: 20 minutes
Cooking time: 10 minutes
Oven: 190°C, 375°F, Gas Mark 5

1. Line a baking sheet with non-stick silicone paper.
2. Cream the margarine and icing sugar together until

smooth. Stir in the flour and cornflour with the vanilla essence.
3. Spoon the mixture into a piping bag fitted with a 1cm (½ inch) star vegetable nozzle. Pipe the mixture in different shapes, i.e. stars, whirls and fingers, on to the lined baking sheet. Decorate with pieces of glacé cherries and angelica.
4. Bake in a preheated oven for 8–10 minutes. Cool on a wire tray.

MAKES ABOUT 14
Nutrition content per serving   Carbohydrate: 11g   Fat: 6g
Fibre: trace   Kilocalories: 96

DERBY CAKES

These cakes are quick and easy to make. They are more like biscuits and keep just as well in an airtight tin. Some people add a good pinch of mixed spice or ground coriander to the mixture.

225g (8oz) plain flour
pinch of salt
100g (4oz) butter or margarine
100g (4oz) soft brown sugar
100g (4oz) currants
1 egg yolk, beaten
about 50ml (2floz) milk

Preparation time: 20 minutes
Cooking time: 15 minutes
Oven: 180°C, 350°F, Gas Mark 4

1. Sift the flour and salt into a mixing bowl. Cut the fat into the flour and rub in with the fingertips until the mixture resembles breadcrumbs. Mix in the sugar and currants. Stir in the egg yolk and sufficient milk to make a stiff dough. Knead until smooth.
2. Roll out on a floured surface to just over 1cm (½ inch) thick. Cut into 5cm (2 inch) rounds. Place on a greased baking sheet.
3. Prick well and bake in a preheated oven for 15 minutes or until set and golden. Cool on a wire tray and store in an airtight tin.

MAKES ABOUT 16
Nutrition content per serving   Carbohydrate: 21g   Fat: 2g
Fibre: 1g   Kilocalories: 140

Clockwise from the top: Honey & orange brandysnaps; Derby cakes; Piped biscuits

CHERRY & WALNUT CRINKLES

These are thin and crunchy. They can be made with coarsely chopped walnuts instead of almonds if preferred, and with candied orange peel instead of cherries.

50g (2oz) butter
50g (2 oz) caster sugar
40g (1½oz) plain flour, sifted
50g (2oz) glacé cherries, coarsely chopped
50g (2 oz) flaked almonds

Preparation time: 15 minutes
Cooking time: 7–8 minutes
Oven: 190°C, 375°F, Gas Mark 5

1. Cream the butter and sugar together until light and fluffy.
2. Work in the flour and cherries and then the flaked almonds.
3. Put teaspoonfuls of the mixture on a greased baking sheet, about 7.5cm (3 inches) apart to allow for spreading, and flatten with a dampened fork.
4. Bake in a preheated oven for 7–8 minutes, until brown.
5. Allow to cool slightly, then remove from the baking sheet with a palette knife and cool on a wire tray. Store in an airtight tin or plastic container.

MAKES ABOUT 12
Nutrition content per serving   Carbohydrate: 9g   Fat: 6g
Fibre: 1g   Kilocalories: 91

CHOCOLATE ALMOND CRESCENTS

These light, crisp biscuits are perfect served with afternoon tea or coffee.

100g (4oz) unsalted butter, at room temperature
40g (1½oz) caster sugar
1 egg yolk
2 teaspoons rum
150g (5oz) plain flour
1 tablespoon cocoa powder
50g (2oz) ground almonds
TO FINISH:
100g (4oz) plain chocolate, melted
50g (2oz) blanched almonds, chopped

Preparation time: 30 minutes, plus cooling
Cooking time: 20–25 minutes
Oven: 180°C, 350°F, Gas Mark 4

1. Cream the butter and sugar together until light and fluffy. Beat in the egg yolk and rum. Sift the flour, cocoa powder and almonds into the bowl and fold into the butter mixture.
2. Mould walnut-sized pieces of the dough into short sausages with tapered ends. Curve into crescents and place on a buttered baking sheet.
3. Bake in a preheated oven for 20–25 minutes or until the crescents are firm and darker in colour. Remove to a wire tray to cool.
4. When cool, dip each tip into the melted chocolate and then into the chopped almonds. Place each crescent on greaseproof paper and leave until the chocolate has cooled and set.

MAKES ABOUT 24
Nutrition content per serving   Carbohydrate: 10g   Fat: 10g
Fibre: 1g   Kilocalories: 133

COCONUT MACAROONS

For lovers of coconut, these macaroons are so simple to make. They're soft and sugary, and children adore them.

1 egg, beaten
50g (2oz) caster sugar
175g (6oz) desiccated coconut

Preparation time: 10 minutes
Cooking time: 20 minutes
Oven: 180°C, 350°F, Gas Mark 4

1. Put the egg in a mixing bowl. Beat in the sugar with a fork, then stir in the coconut.
2. Press the mixture, a few spoonfuls at a time, into a small egg cup, then turn upside down and tap out on to a greased baking sheet to form little mounds.
3. Bake in a preheated oven for about 20 minutes or until golden brown. Remove from the oven and leave to cool for a few minutes before transferring to a wire tray to cool completely.

MAKES ABOUT 15
Nutrition content per serving   Carbohydrate: 8g   Fat: 14g
Fibre: 5g   Kilocalories: 168

Cherry & walnut crinkles (top); Coconut macaroons;
Chocolate almond crescents

GINGER WHIRLS

Once this biscuit mixture is rolled up, it can be wrapped in greaseproof paper and foil and stored in the refrigerator for 2 weeks or frozen for 3 months.

275g (10oz) self-raising flour
1 tablespoon ground ginger
1 teaspoon bicarbonate of soda
75g (3oz) caster sugar
3 tablespoons golden syrup
2 tablespoons black treacle
75g (3oz) butter or margarine, melted
1 egg, beaten
25g (1oz) demerara sugar

Preparation time: 15 minutes, plus chilling
Cooking time: 10–12 minutes
Oven: 180°C, 350°F, Gas Mark 4

1. Sift the flour, ginger and bicarbonate of soda into a bowl. Stir in the caster sugar. Add the syrup, treacle, melted butter or margarine and beaten egg and mix to a soft dough.
2. Knead the dough lightly on a floured surface. Place the dough on a large piece of floured foil or non-stick silicone paper and roll out to form an oblong 30 × 37.5cm (12 × 15 inches).
3. Sprinkle the dough evenly with the demerara sugar. Using the foil or paper to help you, roll up the dough from one long edge. Wrap the dough in the foil or paper and chill for 2 hours.
4. Using a sharp knife, thinly slice off rounds of dough and place, a little apart, on a greased baking sheet.
5. Bake in a preheated oven for 10–12 minutes, until slightly risen. Leave the biscuits on the baking sheets for 5 minutes, then lift with a palette knife and transfer to a wire tray to cool. Once cold, store the biscuits in an airtight tin.

MAKES ABOUT 40
Nutrition content per serving   Carbohydrate: 9g   Fat: 2g
Fibre: 0g   Kilocalories: 54

SPICE BISCUITS

150g (5oz) plain flour
1 teaspoon ground cinnamon
1 teaspoon ground mace
100g (4oz) butter
50g (2oz) caster sugar

Preparation time: 15 minutes
Cooking time: 15 minutes
Oven: 180°C, 350°F, Gas Mark 4

1. Sift the flour and spices together. Cream the butter and sugar together until light and fluffy. Add the flour and mix with your fingertips.
2. Roll out on a floured board to 5mm (¼ inch) thick. Using a 6cm (2½ inch) fluted cutter, cut out 20 rounds. Place on a greased baking sheet and prick with a fork. Bake in a preheated oven for 15 minutes. Cool on a wire tray.

MAKES 20
Nutrition content per serving   Carbohydrate: 9g   Fat: 4g
Fibre: 0g   Kilocalories: 73

SPONGE DROPS

3 tablespoons caster sugar
1 egg (size 1 or 2)
4 tablespoons strong flour, sifted
TO FINISH:
jam, lemon curd or whipped cream
icing sugar

Preparation time: 20 minutes, plus cooling
Cooking time: 8 minutes
Oven: 200°C, 400°F, Gas Mark 6

1. Line a baking sheet with non-stick silicone or greased greaseproof paper.
2. Whisk the sugar and egg together until thick and pale, and the whisk leaves a trail when it is lifted out. (Place the bowl over a pan of hot water if not whisking with an electric beater.) Fold in the flour.
3. Pipe the mixture in small rounds on the lined baking sheet, or use a teaspoon, leaving room for spreading.
4. Bake in a preheated oven for about 8 minutes, until golden. Remove to a wire tray and leave to cool.
5. Sandwich in pairs with jam or lemon curd or whipped cream. Dust with sifted icing sugar.

MAKES ABOUT 12 PAIRS
Nutrition content per serving   Carbohydrate: 5g   Fat: 1g
Fibre: 0g   Kilocalories: 30

Clockwise from the top: Spice biscuits; Sponge drops; Ginger whirls

HAZELNUT & ALMOND BALLS

These petits fours have a crisp sugar coating on the outside. They only need a short cooking time – it can be deceptive cooking chocolate-coloured biscuits, so take care not to overbake as this makes them hard. Should this accidentally happen, leave them exposed to the air for a time and they will become softer.

24 shelled hazelnuts
100g (4oz) ground almonds
100g (4oz) caster sugar
25g (1oz) cocoa powder
1 egg white
50g (2oz) granulated sugar

Preparation time: 30 minutes
Cooking time: 10–15 minutes
Oven: 200°C, 400°F, Gas Mark 6

1. Brown the hazelnuts under a preheated hot grill, shaking the pan frequently. When the skins split and the nuts are lightly coloured, place them in a clean tea towel and rub to remove the skins, which will fall off very easily.
2. Place the ground almonds and sugar in a bowl. Add the cocoa powder and mix well. Add sufficient egg white to bind the mixture together to a slightly soft paste.
3. Divide the paste into portions the size of a walnut and place a hazelnut in the centre of each. Dip first into lightly beaten egg white, then into granulated sugar. Put them on a greased baking sheet.
4. Place in a preheated oven and bake for 10–15 minutes. Cool on a wire tray.

MAKES 24
Nutrition content per serving Carbohydrate: 8g Fat: 6g
Fibre: 1g Kilocalories: 90

SHORTBREAD

175g (6oz) plain flour
50g (2oz) ground rice or rice flour
50g (2oz) caster sugar
100g (4oz) unsalted butter, cut into small pieces
caster sugar, for dredging

Preparation time: 15 minutes
Cooking time: 1 hour
Oven: 170°C, 325°F, Gas Mark 3

1. Butter a 23cm (9 inch) round baking tin.
2. In a bowl, mix the flour, rice and sugar together. Add the butter and knead to a smooth paste.

3. Using the knuckles, spread the mixture evenly to line the bottom of the prepared tin. Using a kitchen knife, divide into 8 wedges, cutting right through to the tin. Prick all over with a fork.
4. Bake in a preheated oven for 1 hour.
5. Remove the biscuits from the tin and cool on a wire tray. Dust with caster sugar before serving.

MAKES 8
Nutrition content per serving Carbohydrate: 29g Fat: 11g
Fibre: 1g Kilocalories: 214

GRASMERE GINGERBREAD

225g (8oz) wheatmeal flour
½ teaspoon bicarbonate of soda
2 teaspoons ground ginger
175g (6oz) butter
175g (6oz) soft light brown sugar
1 tablespoon golden syrup
granulated sugar, for dredging

Preparation time: 15 minutes
Cooking time: 35 minutes
Oven: 170°C, 325°F, Gas Mark 3

1. Sift the flour, bicarbonate of soda and ginger into a bowl. Cut in the butter and rub into the flour with the fingertips until the mixture resembles fine breadcrumbs. Stir in the sugar.
2. Drizzle the syrup into the mixture, stirring all the time, until evenly mixed.
3. Sprinkle the mixture evenly in a 33 × 23cm (13 × 9 inch) shallow oblong tin. Press the mixture down lightly with the back of a metal spoon.
4. Bake in a preheated oven for 35 minutes, until crisp and golden.
5. Sprinkle with sugar, then cut in half lengthways and into three across. Mark each square to make a line through the centre, using a knife. Allow to cool in the tin.
6. When cold, remove and break each piece in half down the marked line.

MAKES 12
Nutrition content per serving Carbohydrate: 28g Fat: 12g
Fibre: 1g Kilocalories: 227

Clockwise from the top: Hazelnut & almond balls;
Grasmere gingerbread; Shortbread

OAT BISCUITS

100g (4oz) plain flour
½ teaspoon salt
100g (4oz) rolled oats
50g (2oz) caster sugar
65g (2½oz) lard or margarine
1 egg, beaten
2–3 tablespoons milk

Preparation time: 20 minutes
Cooking time: 15 minutes
Oven: 180°C, 350°F, Gas Mark 4

1. Sift the flour and salt into a mixing bowl. Mix in the rolled oats and sugar. Cut the fat into the mixture, then rub in with the fingertips until the mixture resembles breadcrumbs. Bind with the beaten egg, adding milk as necessary to make a stiff dough.
2. Roll out thinly on a floured board. With a plain cutter, cut out 6cm (2½ inch) rounds. Place on a greased baking sheet.
3. Bake in a preheated oven for 15 minutes or until crisp and golden. Cool on a wire tray.

MAKES ABOUT 24
Nutrition content per serving   Carbohydrate: 9g   Fat: 3g
Fibre: 0g   Kilocalories: 68

CHOCOLATE RINGS

100g (4oz) butter or margarine, at room temperature
100g (4oz) caster sugar
1 egg (size 4), beaten
drop of vanilla essence
225g (8oz) plain flour
25g (1oz) cocoa powder
2 × 25g (1oz) chocolate flakes
175g (6oz) plain chocolate

Preparation time: 30 minutes, plus chilling
Cooking time: 15 minutes
Oven: 190°C, 375°F, Gas Mark 5

1. Cream the butter or margarine and sugar together until pale and fluffy. Beat in the egg and vanilla essence. Sift the flour and cocoa together and stir into the creamed mixture. Add the crushed flake.
2. Turn out on to a floured surface and knead lightly to a smooth dough. Wrap and chill in the refrigerator for 30 minutes.

3. Roll out the dough to about 5mm (¼ inch) thick on a floured surface. Cut into 5 cm (2 inch) rounds with a plain cutter. Remove the centres with a smaller cutter and place the rings on a lightly greased baking sheet.
4. Bake in a preheated oven for 15 minutes. Leave on the baking sheet for 2 minutes, then remove and cool on a wire tray.
5. Melt the chocolate gently in a small bowl over a pan of hot water. When the biscuits are cold, dip the top of each ring, holding it on a fork, into the melted chocolate and place to set on a sheet of oiled greaseproof paper.

MAKES ABOUT 24
Nutrition content per serving   Carbohydrate: 18g   Fat: 7g
Fibre: 0g   Kilocalories: 135

CORNISH FAIRINGS

These little biscuits were sold at the fairs which were held all over the West Country. There are several kinds but these are the crunchy Cornish variety.

225g (8oz) self-raising flour
1½ teaspoons bicarbonate of soda
pinch of salt
1 teaspoon ground ginger
1 teaspoon mixed spice
½ teaspoon ground cinnamon
100g (4oz) butter or margarine
50g (2oz) caster sugar
100g (4oz) golden syrup

Preparation time: 25 minutes
Cooking time: about 10 minutes
Oven: 190°C, 375°F, Gas Mark 5

1. Sift the flour, bicarbonate of soda, salt and spices into a bowl.
2. Rub in the butter with the fingertips until the mixture resembles breadcrumbs. Stir in the sugar.
3. Heat the golden syrup a little, then pour it into the bowl and knead until it forms a firm dough.
4. Flour your hands and roll the dough into small balls. Put them on a greased baking sheet, well spaced out. Flatten down well with the back of a spoon.
5. Bake in the centre of a preheated oven for about 10 minutes or until golden brown. Remove from the baking sheet and cool on a wire tray.

MAKES ABOUT 30
Nutrition content per serving   Carbohydrate: 10g   Fat: 3g
Fibre: 0g   Kilocalories: 66

Clockwise from the top: Oat biscuits; Cornish fairings; Chocolate rings

INDEX